GW00546092

THE COUNTRYMAN
Companion

Number 3

Edited by Bill Taylor

First published in Great Britain in 2004 by
the Countryman division of
Dalesman Publishing Company Ltd,
Stable Courtyard, Broughton Hall,
Skipton, North Yorkshire BD23 3AZ
www.thecountryman.co.uk

© Dalesman Publishing Company Ltd

A British Cataloguing in Publication record
is available for this book.

ISBN 1 85568 210 9

Printed and bound by Smith Settle, Otley

Contents

Illustrations

Front cover from *Pinewoods
of the Black Mount*
CHRISTOPHER WORMELL

Title page and tailpieces
CHRISTINE ISHERWOOD

Editor's introduction

TWENTY YEARS AGO, THE BBC HAD GARDENERS' QUESTION TIME and *Gardener's World*. There were a couple of good weekly magazines and one or two monthlies, along with some outstanding columnists in the national daily newspapers. Around a third of the fruit and vegetables produced in Britain were grown in home gardens.

Recently, we have seen an enormous increase in the hours of television devoted to gardening and a plethora of titles on every newsagent's shelf, but home fruit and vegetable production has fallen below ten per cent. What happened? Did most of the gardeners just move on to the sofa?

Stefan Buczacki believes that Britain's collective gardening knowledge has slipped. Television and the huge expansion in the gardening industry seem to have done nothing to enhance our 'great strength in depth of gardening knowledge' — quite the reverse.

In some ways, this shouldn't be surprising. Television will always inhabit that borderland where entertainment and education rub shoulders and it should make no apologies for doing so. The fact that the British public now spend several billion pounds a year on gardening is no guarantee of good husbandry, either. Money isn't everything.

Perhaps the truth of this modern morality tale is that

nothing comes easy in gardening, and the idea of the instant garden is beguiling but ultimately a delusion. Growing things takes a lifetime of patience and accumulated knowledge, along with the ability to learn from your mistakes season after season. And these are rather attractive countryside virtues.

I suppose this is what the *Countryman Companion* is all about: a celebration and an exploration of the virtues of a rural way of life, for even in the midst of the city a good garden is always a dream of your own perfect corner of the countryside. This celebration has many facets.

COLIN BECKINGAM is a Hampshire boy who ended up in the wilderness of northern Ontario in Canada. He 'wasted some time in banking and teaching' before giving in to his love of agriculture, horticulture and the countryside. In this issue of the *Countryman Companion*, he explores the huge differences between man's relationship with the wild in England and Canada, a difference that can be life-threatening if you don't understand survival skills.

AMY-JANE BEER grew up in Northern Ireland, Germany and England in a family where long country walks were part of everyday life. As a teenager, she dreamed of a career involving natural history, writing and handsome millionaires. 'Twenty years on, two out of three ain't bad.' Amy has a PhD in biology and is a widely published nature writer. She explores how the current 'look don't touch' approach to natural history is borne out of an understandable desire to protect the environment, but is creating an unhealthy gulf between man and nature.

[8]

INTRODUCTION

STEFAN BUCZACKI is one of Britain's most distinguished gardening experts. He obtained a first in botany at Southampton University and took a postgraduate degree in forest science at Oxford before achieving a global reputation in horticultural research. Stefan now divides his time between writing, broadcasting and his own garden design and consulting practice.

HAZEL CAVENDISH was born in Kenya and her lifelong career in journalism includes spells with Reuters and Lord Beaverbrook's *Daily Express* in Fleet Street. She travelled to the USA in search of the true spirit of Thanksgiving, and came back with a funny and revealing essay on the preservation and hunting of wild turkeys — the same breed that met the Founding Fathers when they landed in the seventeenth century.

DAVID CHAPMAN is an award-winning Cornish writer and photographer with a passion for conserving our wild animals and wild places. He puts his conservation theory into practice on the smallholding which he shares with his wife Sarah. In this issue of the *Companion*, he describes how rare breeds of cattle, sheep and other farm animals are being reintroduced by conservation-minded farmers in an attempt to save our threatened heathlands and marginal sea-pastures.

MATTHEW HOLT abandoned his job in the City in that dangerous time of 'mid-life crisis' and went off to climb Mount Everest. While stuck in a tent on the mountain, he read Jerome K Jerome's *Three Men in a Boat* and decided to

celebrate his survival by rowing down the Thames. He was educated at Cambridge, but didn't row there largely because of the early-morning starts.

CALVIN JONES is a natural history writer who grew up on the north Wales coast, where long days exploring the beaches and rocky shores led to an abiding fascination with the British coastline. It was a fascination that led Calvin to study marine biology at university and then to participate in a long-term rocky shore monitoring project in West Cork, Ireland, where he now lives.

PETER LAING is a retired veterinary surgeon and animal pathologist. He studied at the Royal Veterinary College in London in the late 1940s and worked on the college staff before becoming principal of a run-down rural practice in Herefordshire. His essay is a fond and funny remembrance of his first boss. At a time when fewer and fewer new vets are choosing to join an agricultural practice, it reminds us how important vets are to British farming.

MICHAEL VOCKINS is a man of many parts. He is a free-lance writer and honorary curate of three rural parishes on the north-western slopes of the Malvern Hills. He is also rural dean of Ledbury and for thirty years was secretary (chief executive) of Worcestershire County Cricket Club. For more than twenty years, he and his wife Eileen have lived in Birchwood Lodge, which was Edward Elgar's country retreat and one of the great composer's favourite places.

RICHARD WHEELER is a journalist and photographer with a deep love of the countryside. He was brought up in Herefordshire and went to school near Ludlow and then Malvern College. He is currently writing a book on medieval church screens of the southern Welsh Marches. In this issue of the *Companion*, Richard celebrates some of Britain's surviving small presses that turn publishing into an art form.

BILL TAYLOR
March 2004

MICHAEL VOCKINS

Elgar the countryman

THE UNMISTAKABLY ROUSING GRANDEUR OF THE 'POMP AND
Circumstance Marches', a lusty singing of 'Land of Hope
and Glory' (set to the first of the *Marches*), or the hauntingly moving notes of 'Nimrod' from the *Enigma Variations*
immediately bring to mind England's favourite composer, perhaps its greatest. But would you recognise him as a true countryman, steeped in the countryside and a lover of nature?

Before fame was assured, the often introspective
Edward Elgar feared that the musical establishment per-
ceived him as no more than a provincial musician, a fiddle
player and music teacher. He saw himself as a genuine
countryman. So too did many friends, and those who
came to know him away from his music would have considered him the very reverse of your typical composer.

As success established him as one of Britain's finest
composers and life became kinder, the countryman meta-
morphosed into the country gentleman. He was certainly
someone who, by instinct, was comfortable, and at home

[12]

and at peace, in the countryside. One of his closest friends, W H Reed, described him thus in 1898: 'A very distinguished-looking English country gentleman, tall, with a large and somewhat aggressive moustache, a prominent but shapely nose and rather deep-set but piercing eyes. It was his eyes perhaps that gave the clue to his real personality: they sparkled with humour, or became grave or gay, bright or misty as each mood in the music revealed itself. He looked upstanding, had almost a military bearing ... he was practical to a degree...'

And yet, within that duality of his personality — as countryman and composer — and amidst his introspection was there, too, a sense of his true worth, a clear sense of destiny? As a young boy he had once told his mother that he wouldn't be content until he received a letter from abroad addressed to: Edward Elgar, England.

Elgar was born in 1857, in a humble cottage in the little hamlet of Crown East, Lower Broadheath, from where Worcester's Cathedral and city could be seen across the meadows and where, to the south, the Malvern Hills rear up out of the Severn plain. By the time of his death in Worcester in 1934 — and by then he was Sir Edward Elgar, GCVO, OM, and Master of the King's Musick — Elgar had lived the greatest part of his life on, near, or within sight of his beloved Malvern Hills.

In his lifetime he moved house a good many times, more than twenty moves in all. Some properties were taken on short leases (renting was much more the norm in that period) necessitating a move when a lease elapsed, but some of the Elgars' moves coincided with another success, another achievement. Some, too, were prompted by his wife, Alice, and her undoubted ambitions for her husband. For a period either side of the First World War they lived in London, principally at Hampstead. In 1911 Hampstead had its farms, cattle, and sheep. It was still rural, but not sufficiently so for Elgar: 'I am sick of towns', he wrote in 1916. It was the rural lands of the Worcestershire–Herefordshire border that were his spiritual home. These acres embraced by the Severn, the Wye and the Teme, encircling the Malverns, continued to call to him. Here Elgar was happiest.

Given a choice he would have opted for country life and, probably most of all, for Birchwood. Birchwood is a hamlet at the northern end of the Malverns where the hills drop to 600 feet (180 m) and become the Suckley Hills (a geological distinction lost on both locals and visitors). Surrounded by woods and fields, by peace and tranquility, Birchwood offers breath-takingly beautiful, almost limitless, views over the Severn Valley, to the Clent Hills, Bredon Hill, the Cotswolds, across into Herefordshire and the Welsh Mountains and, of course, to the nearby Malverns and beyond.

Elgar and his wife Alice came to Birchwood Lodge in 1898. The cottage was rented from Squire Little, of Birchwood Hall. A wealthy landowner, it was said that once he had passed Worcester's city boundary, Squire Little could drive all the way home without leaving his own land, a distance of some nine or ten miles (15 km) as the crow flies.

The Elgars used Birchwood Lodge as a retreat until 1903. Here they came, from Malvern, for weekends and for weeks at a time. Elgar could compose without all the distractions that town life created. Often he would work in a frenzied driven way, going for hours without food, working uninterruptedly. Alice's diary recalls: 'E. writing very hard.'; 'E. very engrossed last chorus Gerontius'; 'Nearly finished great chorus.' Those of his works principally associated with Birchwood include one of his *Pomp and Circumstance Marches*, the *Sea Songs* (bar 'Where Corals Lie'), the oratorio *Caractacus* and what many consider as his greatest work of all, *The Dream of Gerontius*.

When his bursts of composition were finished Elgar often felt drained and worn out but the peace and quiet, and the beautiful countryside, of Birchwood exerted their strong restorative powers. And always there were the two Elgars — Elgar the musician and, alongside him, Elgar the countryman. With musical work set aside Elgar the countryman came to the fore.

His love of the countryside was imbibed and nurtured, in part, at an early age, when he accompanied his piano-tuner father to the big country houses. Here, while William Elgar tuned the pianos (sometimes calling Edward to play improvisations and show off his talents, at the same time affirming the efficacy of his own work), young Edward could roam about in their grounds and the surrounding fields. Little from that period slipped from his memory. Mr Elgar, it appears, was not much of a hand at the financial side of his music and piano-tuning business, but he knew how to be a showman, often riding to his tuning appointments on a thoroughbred horse. A love of horses was something else the young Elgar retained all his life.

It is through Edward Elgar's own words, and those of Alice as well as those of friends, that we know of his love of country life. He headed one letter: 'Birchwood Lodge, near Malvern. Saturday, date and month and year unknown 'cos it's Birchwood.' In another he said: 'We came up here two days ago and are in a fog & the leaves are falling too rapidly, but it is jolly nevertheless ...'

An unending delight, which Birchwood gave him, was cycling. Squire Little taught both he and Alice to cycle, in the lane near the cottage. In those final days of the Victorian era learning to ride a bicycle was a serious occupation. On the very day he completed the orchestration of his vast work on *Gerontius*, into which he had poured himself totally, heart and driven soul, Alice recalled: 'We have both been learning to bicycle. E. can now go beautifully and I am just beginning. Our landlord friend and neighbour has been unweariedly teaching us...'

Her words conjure up a picture of a day of wonderful and amazing contrasts. In the morning, carried along by the sublime music pouring from him, and under immense pressure to meet an already delayed and critical deadline, Elgar finished the great chorus of this hauntingly beautiful work. Alice said: 'E. has today finished his orchestration .. he has written his Dream of G. from his very soul.' It was, arguably, the pinnacle of his life's work; certainly so in his own mind for, having added the very last note of the orchestration, Elgar signed off the final page of the score 'Fine' to which he then added a Ruskin quotation: '"This is the best of me; for the rest, I ate, and drank, and slept, loved and hated, like another; my life was as the vapour, and is not; but this I saw and knew; this, if anything of mine, is worth your memory." Edward Elgar, Birchwood Lodge. 3rd August 1900.'

The completion of this work was timely in another sense too. A friend, William Eller, had cycled over from Ledbury to join the Elgars for lunch. And then on this day of mighty achievement Elgar and his wife went out onto the lane to practise their cycling.

The bicycle opened up new vistas for Elgar and there were excursions to Tewkesbury, Hereford, and Evesham, and to the lovely villages surrounding the Malverns. A schoolteacher friend, Rosa Burley, concluded: 'There cannot have been a lane within twenty miles of Malvern that we did not ultimately find. We cycled to Upton, to Tewkesbury, to Hereford, to the Vale of Evesham, to Birtsmorton ... to the lovely villages on the west side of the Hills — everywhere.' Much cycling was done in the company of friends, but walking was often a solitary pastime, especially when it led along the lane from Birchwood to Knightwick and the meadowed banks of the River Teme — a favourite, 'secret', place. This must have reawoken boyhood memories for Elgar, for when he was nine or ten he had been spotted sitting by the river bank with lined music paper and a pencil. In his sixties he himself recalled: 'I am still at heart the dreamy child who used to be found in the reeds by the Severn ... trying to fix the sounds'. From boyhood to his final years the countryside constantly inspired him and, above all, relaxed him, refreshed him, renewed him.

But not all was restful. Elgar liked action too, as another letter describes: 'I was out all day yesterday with a saw mill, sawing timber joists, planks, posts, rafters, boarding! yea boarding with a feather edge: how little ye town folk know of real life.' And alongside all these activities, the cycling and walking, there was potato growing, making paths through the woods surrounding the cottage, searching for snakes, flying kites (a great passion), fishing, and hunting and beagling too. On one occasion a day off fox-hunting meant 'no proof-correcting done'. On another he was 'just off to the beagles & I shall be away all day — no music like the baying of hounds'. Many would readily echo these sentiments but they are words which come especially well from the countryman-composer. Writing to his publisher, who doubtless would have much preferred to hear about the progress of musical work, Elgar said: 'I had friends coming and my brain (?) has been a fog of horse talk, hound jaw, fox gossip and game chatter'. His publisher responded; 'You live too well for a composer, you lucky fellow.' 'I am so madly devoted to my woods', Elgar wrote to a friend. 'I wish you were here! I've been cutting a long path through the dense jungle like primitive man only with more clothes.' To another he told of the young hawks flying about, and plovers and, with the love-hate which many country folk experience, he recounts '150 rabbits under my window and the blackbirds eating the cherries like mad'.

So the country-lover filled his 'free' time at Birchwood. Back at home in Malvern and elsewhere he pursued his love of golf and racing. Another love was dogs. Elgar owned a collie, Scap, in his bachelor years. Scap was a present from Dr Charles Buck, a Yorkshire country doctor, and his wife, and in his correspondence with them Elgar kept the Bucks informed about Scap: 'This morning I had him out at 7.30 into the river and he had his first fight with a Newfoundland brute which began it; no harm done' and

'I took him over to Stoke Prior for the weekend and had a vagabond day on the common after rabbits ..' Alice Elgar did not share her husband's love of dogs but after her death in 1920 he chose once again to have dogs around him and, in the next fourteen years, made up for the abstinence of the previous thirty. Long after Birchwood had

been given up (with the greatest reluctance), and during his London sojourn, the Elgars rented another cottage surrounded by woodland. Brinkwells, near Fittleworth, is deep in the Sussex countryside. Alice, and their daughter Carice, found the cottage, recognising Elgar's need to recapture the peace and solitude which he had so loved, and which had inspired him, at Birchwood. It is with Brinkwells that his beautiful Cello Concerto is linked.

Here he fished in the streams and rivers, walked in the woods among the bluebells, admired the sunrises and listened to the nightingales. He refreshed his carpentry skills, making a stool for a friend and also a table for the summerhouse that he himself had restored. Like many good country folk his life-long habit was to rise early, and be about before the rest of the household stirred. Throughout his life Elgar was moved by scenery and landscape, and by the countryside in all its humours. During a Scottish holiday in Wester Ross, looking across to Skye, he and his daughter, Carice, took a boat out to see the fish, and there, too, he revelled in watching 'gannets, oyster-catchers, divers and a dozen others' feeding their young.

As a young boy he had ridden over the Malvern Hills, sometimes bareback but, surprisingly (considering the times), there is little other record of his riding much, if at all, in later life. Yet his love of horses remained. On the outbreak of war in 1914 he wrote (perhaps over-stressing his fears): 'The only thing that wrings my heart & soul is the thought of the horses — oh! my beloved animals — ... I walk round and round this room cursing God for allowing dumb beasts to be tortured ... oh, my horses.' How his views must have been echoed across the country-side by all who had worked with horses, at the plough or the hay-cart. But let's come back to Birchwood for one more glorious moment. When writing *Gerontius* with its ethereal music, its amazing soaring choruses ('Praise to the Holiest in the height'), he broke off to write to a close friend and in his words the two Elgars — Elgar the great British composer and Elgar the country gentleman with his boundless love of the countryside and especially the woods — came together in the truest and most revealing of heartfelt unity: 'The trees', he said, 'are singing my music, or have I sung theirs?'

AMY-JANE BEER

Getting to grips with nature

'Among scientists are collectors, classifiers,
and compulsive tidiers-up; many are detectives
by temperament and many are explorers; some
are artists and others artisans.'

SIR PETER MEDAWAR, 1915-1987

THE 'LOOK DON'T TOUCH' APPROACH TO WILDLIFE APPRECIATION
has grown out of a very real need to protect the environment and preserve it for future generations to enjoy.
But taken too literally it stifles curiosity and widens the
gulf between ourselves and the natural world. Responsible
natural history collecting can help put us back in touch
with nature.

There's a popular adage in conservation: 'Take nothing
but photographs, leave nothing but footprints'. In some
environments, even footprints are a problem. Research in
the Canyonlands National Park in Utah suggests that a
single human footfall causes damage to the thin soil and

fragile desert plants that takes more than a decade to heal. But this is an extreme example and most habitats, certainly here in Britain, are more than robust enough to withstand the passing of human feet. They'll also cope with moderate responsible collecting.

For generations of children, nature collections were part of growing up — little girls were encouraged to press wild flowers while their male siblings pinned beetles to cards and smuggled frogs in their pockets. Children engaging in such behaviour today might be considered by some to be worryingly deviant. Wildflowers are too precious to pick and who knows what infections or infestations one might contract by handling a wild animal? Why would any child need to go out looking for nature when they have almost unlimited information at their nice clean fingertips in books, on television and on the internet?

In the seventeenth, eighteenth and nineteenth centuries, collecting was an important part of serious nature study. Before the early 1600s, the study of animals and plants had advanced little in two thousand years, and the standard references on natural history still drew heavily on the observations of Aristotle, the Greek philosopher who died in 322 BC. The seventeenth century was a time of huge political and religious upheaval in Britain, with the English Civil War and the subsequent restoration of the monarchy and the rise and fall of Puritanism. It also marked a radical departure in the study of nature and the beginnings of what we now call science.

The English philosopher Francis Bacon advanced the empirical method for studying the world and everything in it. He rejected the scholastic approach that had prevailed throughout medieval history, in which answers to the great questions of life were sought in the teaching of others or by philosophy. Instead Bacon advocated 'taking the question to nature' — in other words, tackling problems by the gathering of data, by observation and by experiment. Bacon was convinced that the application of inductive (scientific) method could be brought to bear on Nature, that her secrets could be 'tortured from her' and that ultimately She could be dominated and controlled — a doctrine most modern scientists would prefer to distance themselves from. Bacon was also a corrupt politician and a misogynist, but nobody is perfect and it is largely thanks to his ideas that the science of natural history was born and that the great era of collecting began.

The new empirical study of the natural world created an incredible thirst for material. For three hundred years collecting has gone hand in hand with exploration, as expeditions set out for newly discovered parts of the world. The names of some of the greatest collectors are the stuff of natural history legend: Henry Walter Bates, Joseph Banks, Henry Morton Stanley, Alfred Russell Wallace, Charles Darwin. And the tradition continues, both on our planet and beyond — in 1969, men brought back samples of moon rock and moon dust, and, courtesy of a busy little robot called *Spirit*, NASA scientists are collecting images and other data from the surface of Mars even as I write.

One of the great things about collecting is the longevity it gives to specimens that would otherwise wither, fade, erode or generally go the way of all things. Sir Hans Sloane formed the basis of the natural history collection at the British Museum and later the Natural History

Museum in London. The latter now boasts one of the largest natural history collections in the world, with an estimated 70 million preserved specimens including 800,000 'types'. Type specimens are those from which a species is described and with which subsequent similar discoveries must be compared before they can be allocated to the same species or deemed different enough to warrant the creation of a new group, for which they will become the type specimen.

During the eighteenth and nineteenth centuries, as awareness of the wondrous diversity of life began to develop, natural history collecting became a popular hobby among the well off. Gentleman naturalists amassed huge collections of pinned butterflies, carefully blown birds'

eggs and stuffed animals. Often the actual collecting was done by commercial operators and there was a handsome living to be made in the buying and selling of various treasures of nature. Today such activities are often regarded as little more than the plundering of the Earth's natural heritage and collectors face anything from disapproving glares to criminal prosecution.

But collecting does not have to be damaging, and there is no need for all collectors to be tarred with the same brush as those sad individuals hell-bent on owning or trading rare natural artefacts, whatever the consequence. The Society for the Preservation of Natural History Collections defines collecting as 'the process of sampling the natural and cultural world using a variety of techniques'. In its loosest sense, this could mean taking a photograph, a sketch or simply making a list of what you see in a particular place. Birdwatchers are thus collectors of records; photographers and artists are collectors of landscapes. Then there is the more traditional definition, whereby collecting means physically removing something from one place in order to store or use it elsewhere.

Collecting is still an important part of science, but it is much more carefully regulated than ever before. Since the 1992 Rio Convention on Biodiversity, signatory nations have undertaken to share knowledge and specimens from their existing collections so that natural resources can be spared.

So when, where and what is it all right to collect? It is perfectly possible to make collections without denuding the natural environment or harming wildlife. As a general rule if an object is past its original usefulness, it's probably

okay. Just as collectors of antiques and other knick-knacks pick through bric-a-brac and junk shops looking for a bargain, the naturalist can rummage though Nature's jumble sale and come up with a wealth of cast-off treasures no longer required by their original owner — empty shells, abandoned nests, cast antlers, moulted feathers and so on. If the object is one of many, make a note of the others and take just one. If it's something very unusual, large or potentially valuable, you should contact an appropriate organisation to report your find — this applies particularly to fossils.

While there is no law in Britain forbidding their collection, you would be on dodgy ground if you were caught trying to chisel a significant find out of a piece of private land, nature reserve or other protected site. On the other hand, responsible collecting of fossils can be an important aspect of geological conservation and highly beneficial to science, especially at sites where there is a rapid rate of erosion or degradation, such as sea cliffs or active quarries. Fossils left *in situ* in such places will soon be lost forever. On the whole, UK conservation organisations actively encourage fossil collecting, as long as it is done properly. For further information, contact English Nature, Scottish Natural Heritage or the Countryside Council for Wales. The Palaeontological Association or the Geologists Association are also useful points of contact.

Fossil hunting is one of two acceptable forms of natural history collecting for which there is a clear code of practice. The other is fungi. In both cases the recommendations are to respect the rights of landowners, never to collect more than you need, avoid collecting anything that is rare, avoid causing damage to the habitat or other wildlife, and record any significant finds. Such common sense recommendations will stand you in good stead for all types of natural history collecting.

Three pieces of legislation the amateur collector should be aware of are the Theft Act of 1968, the Wildlife and Countryside Act of 1981 and the Wild Birds Protection Act of 1954. The first two forbid the digging up and removal of wild plants (including fungi) without permission of the landowner. The collection of most wild foods from public land for personal consumption is legal but amassing wild fruits, nuts, flowers, or fungi for personal commercial gain is not. The Wildlife and Countryside Act provides additional protection for rare plants and animals — and it is illegal to damage or harm these wherever they are. This includes picking flowers, taking cuttings or interfering with the nests or homes of birds and animals. It is illegal to collect the eggs of most wild bird species, or to possess them without a licence. The law on egg collecting dates back fifty years to the Wild Birds Protection Act 1954, while possession was outlawed by the Wildlife and Countryside Act 1981. The penalties for egg collecting crimes are potentially severe — up to a £5,000 fine or six months in prison per egg. And yet, sadly, the RSPB estimate there are still around 300 active collectors in the UK and they remain a significant threat to some of our rarest and most treasured bird species — the osprey, sea eagle, red kite, and Slavonian and black-necked grebes.

As to where you can collect, some guidelines are provided by the law and by various authorities responsible for land management — for example private landowners, the National Trust or National Park Authorities. In most other places, moderate collecting of dead material from non-protected species for non-commercial purposes is perfectly legal. However, you should check local bylaws first and bear in mind that areas designated as Sites of Special Scientific Interest or National Nature Reserves often have stricter regulations.

When to collect and when to leave be is really a question of common sense. Abundance isn't necessarily the best guide. I remember a spring afternoon in Northern Ireland in 1976, when my mum took my little sister and me to a wooded hillside close to our house. The steeply sloping ground was a breathtaking violet haze of bluebells, shimmering in the May sunshine. On our way up the sandy path we met a couple of older children. Each of them was laden with two whole armfuls of flowers. They must have been carrying seven or eight hundred stems each and neither had a hand free to fend off the small squadron of avid bees that pursued them. At five years of age, I realised the blooms wouldn't last and I was horrified at the pointless overexploitation. As I saw it, the bees only wanted their flowers back. I knew picking so many was wrong, and I'm sure the older children knew it too.

My point is that and that drawing a line between responsible collecting and plunder is really not difficult. If in doubt, ask a five-year-old. Their simplistic view of right and wrong, plus their natural curiosity and eye for small details make them great collectors.

Having covered the questions of what and where — how about why? What is the point of collecting anyway? After all, you're unlikely to come across a new species in our heavily studied countryside, and if all one is allowed to collect these days are bits of dead animals and plants that aren't worth anything, why bother at all? Many natural collectibles have an undeniable aesthetic quality — antlers, feathers and shells all make very fine displays — but not many people would regard a selection of owl pellets or broken nut shells as things of beauty. To the naturalist, however, such pocketable treasures can be highly significant.

As any collector will tell you, the value of any object is greatly enhanced by a reliable provenance, or information about its history. It is this kind of information that turns a mere accumulation of objects into a real collection. Natural history is no different although the value of collections lies not in the price they might fetch at auction, but in what can be learned from them. If you want your collection to be anything more than an exercise in

hoarding, you'll need to keep records. They answer questions like: what is the object (to the best of your knowledge)? Who found it? Where was it found? Describe the location (eg under a hedge on the north edge of such and such a wood) and note the habitat type. If possible note a grid reference. When was it found? Give the date, season, and time of day. Note any other information you think might be relevant including factors you think might have contributed to the position or condition of your find. For example, recent heavy frosts, droughts, strong winds, or high tides or disturbance such as harvesting, hedge trimming, hunting, forestry or other management. It's pretty much impossible to record too much information.

Once you've accumulated records of this sort, it's pretty pointless keeping them to yourself. Your local Wildlife Trust will be able to put you in touch with an appropriate records centre where information about your collection can be turned into useful data. Alternatively you can contact an appropriate organisation from the list given at the end of this article. Not only will they be interested in positive sightings of animals and plants, they can also use records of animal signs such as tracks, nests and feeding remains. No record is too small, and no species of wild animal is too common or mundane. The records officer of my local Mammal Group has been collecting data about mammals in Yorkshire for thirty years. In all that time he received just one record of a house mouse. Clearly this does not reflect reality. It's easy enough to understand why people don't bother to report sightings of common animals, but unless they do, trends in the fortunes of such animals can be very difficult to spot. Who would have thought ten years ago that the house sparrow was about to become one of Britain's fastest declining birds? Perhaps if more people routinely recorded the appearance of birds in their gardens we would have recognised the trend sooner, instead of waiting for a vague collective realisation that those little dusty brown fellas aren't as common as they were.

Plant records are useful in the same way, and if you need convincing that amateur records really do count, look no further than the *New Atlas of the British and Irish Flora*, published in 2002 by English Nature. This landmark publication gives up to date information regarding the distribution of nearly 3,000 species of plant in the British

Isles. Collecting the mass of information required for the book involved the efforts of 1,600 field botanists, most of them volunteers.

The point I'm trying to make is that natural history collecting need not be disreputable, nor is it old fashioned. I'm not advocating pinning butterflies to cards, pickling frogs, or shimmying up trees to collect birds' eggs. Except in limited research situations, this is of little benefit to science or nature. But nor do I want to see the countryside turned into a museum in which we tread carefully on authorised paths, solemnly looking but not touching the exhibits and missing out on all that goes on just beyond our gaze. Don't be afraid to get to grips with nature — you might be amazed at what you discover from the contents of your pockets and the scribblings in your notebook when you get home.

Useful organisations:
Tracking Mammals Partnership: www.trackingmammals.org.uk
British Trust for Ornithology: www.bto.org.uk; tel 01842 750050
English Nature: www.english-nature.org.uk; tel 01733 455000
Scottish Natural Heritage: www.snh.org.uk; tel 0131 447 4784
Countryside Council for Wales: www.ccw.gov.uk
Geologists' Association: www.geologist.demon.co.uk; tel 020 7434 9298
Palaeontological Association: www.palass.org.uk.

PETER LAING

All vets great and small

MY OLD FRIEND THE PROFESSOR OF VETERINARY MEDICINE gave me a very direct look over his beer as we discussed my forthcoming work as an external lecturer in farm animal pathology. 'Don't expect many of the students to be all that interested in what you're telling them', he said. 'Fewer than ten per cent of them have any intention of having anything to do with agricultural practice after they qualify. It's very different from our day.'

It certainly was, I thought. When I qualified in the 1950s, agriculture in Britain was vitally important. The key position the veterinary profession played in its success was taken for granted and we were all justifiably proud to be part of the system. And we all had such fun!

My mind and memory carried me away back to my first job and my first boss, Joe Holmes, who was principal of the in-house practice at the Royal Veterinary College in Wallingford.

———

Joe picked up the phone. 'Wallingford 2148', he said, his small ginger moustache bristling and his bright blue eyes blinking repeatedly through his round spectacles as he listened. He turned to me as he put down the receiver.

'You can go and see that cow', he said. 'It sounds like an acetonaemia, but make up your own mind and don't forget to do a rectal.'

I soon learnt that being a newly qualified vet was really like being an apprentice and that my boss was as eccentric as he was knowledgeable. On my first morning Joe welcomed me warmly. 'Well, my boy, get your boots and a calving smock', he said, peering hard at me, missing nothing, while at the same time gathering together a pile of equipment and finishing a piece of rather stale-looking toast. 'We'll do today's round together.'

We set off in his old Hillman car and he immediately started an exposition on the first case we were visiting. As he spoke he became increasingly excited, only occasionally concentrating on the road ahead and turning full face towards me as he made each point, changing gear to emphasise its importance so that we progressed along the quiet Oxfordshire roads in a series of swoops.

Once we had seen and treated the cow of our first call, the progress to our next case was even more zany. Joe gave a re-run of the process he had gone through during his examination, changing gear as before as he explained the significance of each clinical point. Then when at last he arrived at his final diagnosis he pulled the gear lever completely out of its socket and waved it triumphantly as he described possible false conclusions he could have reached, before stuffing it back into its socket just seconds before we came to a blind corner where he really did need to change gear.

Experience came quickly and now, a bare six weeks after qualifying, I felt surprisingly confident and able to cope.

Joe was a superb diagnostician as well as a compulsive and brilliant teacher and the warmth of his personality transcended every eccentricity. Egalitarian to a fault, he treated everyone the same and in an age that was still fairly hierarchical, he identified with and became the friend of all the stockmen in the practice. If he ran into difficulties in explaining what he wanted to a cowman or met with any suspicion or reserve, he would stride into a corner and pee against the cowshed wall, turning his head at the same time to peer directly at the surprised cowman. When we were back in the car after one such episode, he explained: 'There's nothing like the passing of water for breaking down social barriers, my boy. You just remember that.' He changed gear to emphasise the point.

One Sunday morning about a month after I had started working at the practice, the telephone rang as I was finishing breakfast in the digs I shared with Bill, the other assistant and a veteran a whole year my senior. It was Gertie Holmes, Joe's wife.

'There's a case for you near Watlington, Peter', she said. 'And Joe wants to see you to tell you about it before you go.'

As I left a few minutes later Bill gave me a wry grin. 'You're in for your Sunday initiation experience now!'

When I pushed open the door at Joe's house the kitchen was full of smoke, as it usually seemed to be. Gertie, motherly and shapeless, smiled to me vaguely from in front of the gas cooker from which smoke was rising in acrid clouds from hot bacon fat and burning toast. 'Joe's in the bath', she said. 'He said you were to go straight up.'

The bathroom door was wide open and wisps of steam were eddying from it across the landing. Rather dubiously I went in. It was a large room painted a dreary dark green, with uncurtained mullioned windows. It had clearly been a bedroom when the old house had still been a farm. In the centre a single electric light bulb dangled over an enamel bath with a cane chair beside it. On the chair was the *News of the World*, a half-full mug of tea and a pair of spectacles.

'Ah, there you are my boy', he said, brandishing a loofah and peering up at me myopically. 'I want to tell you about this case before you set off. It could be tricky.'

Joe, as ever completely unselfconscious, presented a picture never to be forgotten. A lock of his thinning sandy hair had fallen forward into a little curl above one eye, his face was pink and cherubic above his equally pink shoulders and chest and his moustache bristled cheerfully. He leant forward, picked up the mug of tea and took a long gulp.

'I always read the *News of the World* in the bath on Sunday mornings.' he said. 'It's the only place I can get away from the telephone. Now, this cow you're going to see ...'

And he went on to give a minute description of every condition it could possibly be, periodically emphasising a detail by pointing the loofah threateningly at me or sloshing water over his face and blowing out his cheeks.

The first time I was invited for Sunday lunch was also bizarre. Bill and I arrived together and as we opened the door the clouds of smoke were even more dense than usual. Bill took a saucepan of potatoes that had boiled dry off the gas and called through to the drawing room.

'Gertie! There seems to be a bit of a problem in the

kitchen. Can you come through?' Gertie appeared, quite untroubled as usual.

'Oh dear', she said mildly, flapping at the smoke ineffectually with a tea towel, 'Everything was just ready when the telephone rang. Joe's had to go out to Mrs Woodward's. One of her Jerseys is calving.'

We finally sat down for the meal with the Holmes's three children. The eldest girl, just fifteen, ogled Bill and me throughout the meal, giggling and making silly teenage talk. The boy was full of sarcastic comments about the food, but helped himself to very large helpings of everything, even the horrible burnt potatoes. Janet, the younger girl, kept up an endless precocious chatter that made any other conversation impossible. Gertie drifted vaguely in and out of the dining room but didn't sit down with us at all. Joe appeared just as we were leaving to go back to our digs. 'I hope you've had a good meal', he said cheerfully. 'I got her a live calf. Good thing I went quickly, it was a breech. Gert, is there anything left to eat? See you in the morning, boys.'

Mrs Woodward, the owner of the Jersey cows, was a big booming tweedy woman who owned a small country estate near Wallingford and also kept horses and dogs. She was dominating and intolerant and on the frequent occasions when she needed veterinary advice demanded immediate attention from Joe personally as her right. She would only, with very bad grace, consider seeing Bill if there were absolutely no alternative and as junior assistant she did not recognise me as being a vet at all. Joe was greatly in awe of her but there was one memorable Saturday afternoon when he lost patience as he spotted her arriving unexpectedly without an appointment. He was on the point of going out to see Janet run in her school sports day when she started to bang imperiously on the front door.

'Tell her I'm out, Gert. She'll have to see Bill', he said. 'I promised Janet I'd be there for her race. I'll get out round the back where she can't see me.'

But Mrs Woodward was not satisfied. 'I'll wait for Mr Holmes', she boomed. 'He can't be far away. I saw his car as I came in.'

She stumped off round the house and got to the back just as Joe's legs were emerging through the downstairs cloakroom window.

'Ah, there you are, Mr Holmes', she boomed, quite unfazed. 'I knew I'd find you somewhere. I want you to look at my dog Talisman. He's been sick; he's in my car.'

Joe, as Reader in Medicine, had been in charge of the Royal Veterinary College's small animal clinic in London before he was appointed as principal of the college practice. In the 1950s there were not many country vets who had any real expertise in treating dogs and cats, and a large number of people came to the practice with their pets. Wallingford was not far away from the fashionable part of Thames Valley around Maidenhead, and Joe had a significant number of ardent fans among the wealthy ladies who lived in that area. One day after morning surgery Bill was planning his round and had included a visit to a lady near Marlow whose Pekinese was ill. Joe was checking his list before he set off when he spotted the proposed visit. 'Oh no, my boy!' he said, his moustache starting to bristle enthusiastically, 'You can't go there, you're much too young! Mrs Dupont will still be in bed and she keeps the Peke between her breasts. I shall have to go myself.'

The practice and his family were Joe's whole life.

He and Gertie included all of us, and the clients too. We were all always treated with the same open-hearted generosity and commitment. When Gertie died many years later, leaving Joe on his own for the first time since he was a very young man, letters of sympathy and affection came from every assistant that had ever worked in the practice, and many of us came spontaneously to the unpretentious funeral in the little village near Wallingford where she and Joe had unselfishly allowed us to share their lives and where we had all been privileged to learn so much.

All those years later, when I pushed open the door into the lecture theatre and looked across at the rows of intelligent faces — many more girl students than men by now — I thought it must surely be part of my job to bring to them a little of the flavour of Joe Holmes' very special veterinary life.

Footnote: J W H Holmes qualified as a veterinary surgeon in Edinburgh in 1927. He was appointed principal of the Royal Veterinary College practice in Wallingford in 1945. Towards the end of the 1950s, the college completed its final move to its present location within London University at Potters Bar and Joe bought the practice at Wallingford. He continued to practice there until he retired, shortly before his death in 1985.

DAVID CHAPMAN

Traditional breeding matters

MANKIND HAS BEEN MEDDLING WITH THE ENVIRONMENT FOR millennia. Unfortunately, during the twentieth century, our ability to manipulate the environment has increased at a speed greater than our ability to control ourselves with rational thought. Heavy machinery performs the high-impact work while artificial fertilisers, herbicides and insecticides nag away at the health of our ecosystems. Through, at first, need and then subsidy we have tried to convert every small part of our surroundings into fertile, productive land for crops or livestock. Shocked by the effects of these changes during the latter part of the twentieth century, conservationists began to raise the alarm.

Through some of our more historical tinkering with the landscape we accidentally created a greater diversity of habitats than existed before. This was a definite advantage to our natural history. Grassland and heathland are two classic examples of the valuable habitats that were originally created by people. However, in more recent times a great deal of our heathland in lowland Britain has been ploughed up for agriculture to satisfy the growing demands for food in and after the Second World War. On top of this, much of the old and valuable flower-rich grass-land was 'improved' by the introduction of clover and the liberal use of fertilisers and herbicides; these 'improvements' in an agricultural sense led to a sudden decrease in the value of the environment for our wildlife. By the overuse of chemicals we have encouraged the growth of one or two species at the expense of everything else that used to exist in the meadows and heaths. This situation is exacerbated by the fact that it takes such a long time for flowering plants and their associated wildlife to re-colonise areas of grassland so the conservation of existing areas is essential.

Thankfully, though few and far between, most of the high quality examples of these types of habitat are now protected by law and many are nature reserves. They have been saved from the plough, but that doesn't guarantee that their value will survive. It has long been recognised that if left to their own devices grassland and heathland revert to scrub and then woodland, the climax community. Conservation groups, needing to tackle the encroachment of scrub, have relied to some extent upon voluntary work. By bribing a few bearded blokes and woolly-hatted women to wander around in wellies for the day with no more than the promise of inner peace, a bonfire and a few baked potatoes they have kept our nature reserves clear. I have to admit there is nothing quite as exhilarating as a day spent in the field wielding a billhook, but even if this strategy were secure in the long term it wouldn't be ideal since cutting and mowing, in this way, actually favours certain types of plants at the expense of others.

The answer to our predicament has been literally staring us in the face for centuries but has been drifting further away from our consciousness over the last few decades. It's time to look back in history and learn from our ancestors; to remember that both heathland and some types of grassland were formed by our use of domesticated livestock. When I refer to livestock I'm not talking about the milk-making machine which we call the Friesian or the rather bland pork producing pig so aptly named the Large White. These breeds, selected over centuries for specific qualities and purposes, breeds of which Robert Bakewell would have been proud, are of little use on such unimproved land. What we need are the sturdy old breeds common before genetically modified animals became acceptable in the eighteenth century.

The traditional breeds were abandoned by farmers because they didn't provide as much meat or milk or both. Since farmland was becoming more fertile we didn't need to continue farming low productivity animals, so newer breeds became used almost exclusively. In the period between 1900 and 1973 more than twenty breeds of British farm animals became extinct. We became unable to graze heathland and poorer pasture so these areas were deserted by farmers and are now the focus of conservation efforts. With the knowledge that grazed grassland, or pasture, encourages a different selection of plants to the mown meadow we can, and must, select the appropriate conservation strategy for each area. Plants such as plantain and cowslip, with basal rosettes, escape grazing and

so flourish in pasture whereas taller species which cannot survive trampling survive better in grassland which is mown each year.

Rare breeds may not be everyone's cup of tea. You could be forgiven for thinking that the Grazing Animals Project's quarterly magazine is just cannon fodder for the teams featuring on *Have I Got News for You*, but I think you will find that keeping rare breeds is becoming distinctly trendy with your land-owning green-wellied fashion setters. As well as being hardier creatures, capable of eking out an existence on less fertile land, they also provide meat and wool of a higher standard than modern equivalents. In my home county of Cornwall rare breeds are becoming quite common, if that isn't a contradiction in terms. Encouraged by grants available from English Nature to introduce traditional breeds onto grassland areas with conservation value many landowners are now catching on to the benefits. The National Trust, which manages large sections of the Cornish coast, has embraced the 'Traditional Breeds Incentive' in a big way.

Somehow it seems wholly appropriate that, in a county where Bronze Age field systems still exist, we should be welcoming traditional breeds of cattle and sheep. On the coast between Gurnard's Head, originally known as Innyall or desolate place, and Bosigran Head, with its remains of an Iron Age cliff castle, Manx Loghtan sheep graze the boulder-strewn coastal heath. Despite their name they look entirely in keeping with their surroundings. The rams in particular are rugged and robust with four horns giving the impression of a goat rather than a sheep. In keeping with their wild appearance they are shy creatures preferring to melt into the landscape rather than making a show of themselves.

Since the end of the nineteenth century, when the final demise of the boom and bust tin mining industry of Cornwall was on the cards, the coast of the county has suffered serious neglect. Most of the grazing that was carried out on the maritime grass and heathland ceased during, or soon after, the time of the Second World War. Since then the Atlantic has been the only force inhibiting the growth of scrub by providing a regular dose of salt spray which has favoured the small springtime flowers capable of surviving in this difficult habitat. Gradually, though, the lack of grazing has allowed the encroachment of gorse

[47]

and bracken even where the soil has been poisoned by the heavy metals of mining waste.

At the most westerly tip of our land between Land's End and Cape Cornwall lies the valley of Nanquidno. Jutting out into the Atlantic to the north of the valley is the headland of Maen Dower and it is between here and Polpry Cove further to the north that the National Trust is working with their tenant farmer on a scheme to graze this coastal fringe. This area of maritime heath amounts to only around forty-three acres (17 ha), but it is just a very small part of a huge stretch of the coast, between St Ives and a point near Land's End, all of which has been designated as an Environmentally Sensitive Area (ESA). The breed selected here is the Longhorn Cattle, in some ways a strange irony since it was with this breed that Robert Bakewell began experimental breeding in the eighteenth century.

The only reason why this huge section of coast has remained in such outstanding condition is the poor quality of its soil, its depth so shallow that it cannot be ploughed without being washed away. In recent years bracken and gorse have begun to out-compete the spring flowers and so the longhorns were brought in. By a combination of grazing and trampling they opened up sections of the ground to the sunlight and started to redress the balance of nature. They won't ever clear all the scrub but then that is not the aim of the operation. Diversity is the name of the game. Once the flowers are blooming the insects will be back and then the birds; insects need shelter and birds need nest sites so some scrub is of great value.

The project here started just two years ago and it wouldn't be fair to expect a significant change in that

time, so the results have given the National Trust a pleasant surprise. In the very first spring a carpet of bluebells was flowering in the sections opened up to the sunlight. Bluebells are more often associated with woodland but the coast of the south-west has internationally important numbers of coastal bluebells. Other flowers that flourished included: thrift, sea campion, hairy bird's-foot trefoil (another rarity), spring squill, kidney vetch and the very delicate heath-spotted orchid. All in all a magnificent show of colour and scent which also had a positive effect on the number of insects present.

During the second year numbers of breeding birds were up, with linnets seeming to take advantage of the increase in seeds and stonechats feeding on the insects. It is still early days and it would be easy to overstate the successes.

The National Trust still have to learn from their mistakes, but for now it is reassuring to know that the welfare of an increasing number of our valuable conservation sites is in the hands of the creatures that have looked after them for the majority of the last three thousand years. The pedigree of these animals is too long and their value too great for us to allow them to plunge into extinction.

Organisations:
The National Trust are better known for their protection of historical houses but their work on conservation is of great value. Visit their website for information about membership and sites of interest: www.nationaltrust.org.uk.

The Grazing Animals Project (GAP) was formed in 1997 to promote the development of conservation grazing throughout the UK. This project is funded by English Nature and managed by the Wildlife Trusts. GAP helps to establish local grazing schemes providing information, support and networking through newsletters and their website. Contact details: tel. 01636 670095, website www.grazinganimalsproject.org, email gap@cix.co.uk.

English Nature is the government body for environmental protection, they provide grants to support the use of traditional breeds in grazing Sites of Special Scientific Interest (SSSIs). Contact details: 01733 455100, website www.english-nature.org.uk.

The Wildlife Trusts are organised at county level to promote the conservation of natural history and can often give advice about related issues. Contact details: tel. 01636 677711, website www.wildlifetrusts.org.

The Rare Breeds Survival Trust is a group which aims to promote the use of traditional breeds for whatever purpose; website www.rbst.org.uk.

Further reading:
Local Grazing Schemes: a best practice guide. Free from GAP office, tel 01636 670095.
The Breed Profiles Handbook, £15 from English Nature, tel 0870 1214177.
The Lowland Grassland Management Handbook, £22 from the Wildlife Trusts, tel 01636 677711.

TRADITIONAL BREEDING MATTERS

Objectives of the Traditional Breeds Incentive:
To secure wildlife conservation and associated environmental benefits by grazing SSSI land with traditional breeds of cattle sheep and ponies.

To contribute towards the viability of extensive animal production systems (small numbers of animals grazing the land) where there is an appreciable benefit to the nature conservation management.

To promote the genetic conservation of endangered native breeds.

To achieve a high level of management and countryside care on a whole farm basis. *English Nature, 2002.*

Around the Country:
Hebridean sheep are being used by Nottinghamshire Wildlife Trust in Sherwood Forest; their light weight and small feet help to minimise damage.

Belted Galloway cattle are grazing the Wiltshire Wildlife Trust reserve at Jones's Mill near Pewsey.

Highland Cows and Soay sheep are grazing the coastal heath between Kynance Cove and Mullion in Cornwall on behalf of English Nature.

Pygmy and Lynton goats graze the chalk slopes of Betchworth Quarry in Surrey. Water Buffalo keep the waterways of Cilgerran Teifi Marshes, in Cardigan, clear of encroaching weed.

Gloucester Old Spot (cross) pigs are used to clear brambles at Treswell Wood in Nottinghamshire.

Hebridean sheep are used to graze the rank grassland of the National Nature Reserve at Lindisfarne, Northumberland, by English Nature.

It should be noted that the animals are not left on site throughout the whole year, so before making a visit specifically to see them, check with the relevant organisation.

STEFAN BUCZACKI

Good teeth aren't enough

WHEN I WAS ABOUT TO GO IN FRONT OF THE MICROPHONE TO record my first *Gardeners' Question Time* programme, one of my fellow panellists — the late and utterly wonderful Bill Sowerbutts, who was approaching the end of his radio career — gave me a piece of well-worn but salutary advice. I'm not sure in retrospect if it was the best thing to say at the last possible moment to an inexperienced broadcaster making an early venture onto the big stage, but Bill never was one for subtleties. The pointed advice he gave was: 'I'll tell you something lad; you can't flannel with this lot. They'll see through you straight away'.

And how true that was, 'this lot' being the British gardening public who listened to the programme. Anything said on *Gardeners' Question Time* that carried the merest whiff of evasiveness, that gave the slightest indication you didn't know what you were talking about, would be pounced on. The inevitable response from 'disgusted of Tunbridge Wells' would be in the post the next morning.

And with good reason. I said then and I said many times later that I believed there was a greater strength and depth of gardening knowledge, and far more good gardens, in this country than anywhere else. But is this still true? In some respects I don't think it is. I think our collective national gardening know-how has slipped. Yet the gardening industry is now huge, expanding at the rate of about twenty per cent per year and with a retail value of over £5 billion.

My *Gardeners' Question Time* career with Bill Sowerbutts, Clay Jones and Geoffrey Smith began in 1982. At the time there were a couple of good weekly gardening magazines, one or perhaps two monthlies. There was *Gardeners' World* on television presented by the splendid Geoff Hamilton (with whom I sometimes appeared and sometimes disagreed but always respected for his gardening acumen), there were some outstanding gardening columnists in the national newspapers and no internet. Around one third of fruit and vegetables produced in Britain was grown in home gardens, the rose was the most popular flower and many gardeners budded their own.

Now, gardening photographs leap from a plethora of covers on every newsagent's bookshelf (although gardening features are often written by jobbing journalists), home (and garden) ownership has never been higher, there are entire television channels almost devoted to gardening programmes and dozens of gardening websites while gardening books are among the reliable stand-bys of illustrated book publishers. But home garden fruit and vegetable production has fallen below ten per cent, seed sales have slipped, specialist nurseries are in decline, roses have fallen from favour and far from budding a hybrid tea, most gardeners today don't even know how to prune a wisteria. What has happened?

The nursery has given way to the garden centre which is too often simply part of yet another suburban retail park offering 'a day out for the family' and where a significant proportion of the goods on offer seems to amount to dross dressed up in a garden setting; far too many of the specialist plant suppliers have fallen under the juggernaut of the hardy stock production factories of Holland and Belgium; and the gardeners who watch and read the media's output either don't listen to the advice being given; or the advice isn't there. I strongly suspect the latter. It's largely the media itself I blame and I think the situation will become worse because I believe a marvellous opportunity has probably been missed.

Four or five years ago I wrote that the overall standard of gardening programmes on television was generally doing little to arrest the decline in gardening knowledge and expertise in the population at large. At the time I wrote it, gardening was experiencing an unprecedented popularity with television commissioning editors and there were more gardening programmes than ever before. Unfortunately few of them offered authoritative horticulture and were of the style of *Ground Force*, *Flying Gardener*, *Front Gardens*, *Garden Invaders*, and *Planet Patio* (although I never did discover what 'Planet Patio' meant). They used every possible production device to package gardens, gardening and garden design. It may have been great television and terrific fun but meaningful horticulture it wasn't. In some instances, the presenters (the 'gardener' or the 'expert' has largely been replaced by the 'presenter') were well trained and knowledgeable horticulturists but were doing little more than play-acting.

The television landscape has however now changed and gardening has given way to a new genre; of programmes that in an entertaining but rather well informed way (just the thing so much of the gardening output lacked) tell you how to make more money from selling your house. We are left with a handful of gardening productions, including the so-called flagship programme *Gardeners' World* which at a time when we need a new Percy Thrower, Arthur Billitt, Geoffrey Smith or Geoff Hamilton has as its main 'presenter' someone with no proper professional horticultural experience or qualifications whatever. Oh dear.

I am sometimes asked if people with real qualifications, expertise and experience are truly necessary to encourage and guide the public into the practice and enjoyment of gardening. Some television folk point to other areas of interest and entertainment such as cookery and home decorating where they say the moderately enthusiastic and minimally experienced amateur is good enough. But that highlights part of the problem with gardening television. It's been its misfortune invariably to be linked with cooking and decorating as a purely lifestyle subject rather than with documentary topics like history, natural history and archaeology. They too have considerable television air-time and many popular programmes are made around them. Some are serious and academic, some less so, but no-one makes them appear ridiculous and feels the need to turn them into comedy. And to be fair, nor do the current 'home improvement' programmes treat their subject in the same flippant way that gardening has had to endure.

Yes, genuine expertise does matter because without a bedrock of real knowledge and experience, the presenter is reduced to mouthing well-rehearsed words put there by a script consultant or researcher. If they are lucky and the presenter has a kindly smile and personality (although a good voice seems long ago to have been discarded as of any worth in British broadcasting), they might even sound plausible. But time and again, I see non-expert presenters breaking the first rule of television presentation: don't tell the viewers what they can see — amplify and explain it. For example, try watching a non-expert presenter sowing parsley. As he does so, he will tell you he is sowing parsley. Not much help there. He might tell you he is sowing it thinly. We can see that. He might tell you he is adding a little lime to the soil. We can see that too. What he won't tell you is why he has chosen a particular variety of parsley, why he is sowing thinly, why he is adding lime, or anything else of 'added value' about parsley. And the chances are he won't tell you because he doesn't know; and he doesn't know because he himself has never been taught.

There's also a strong likelihood that there will be no-one else present to correct him although I was told a little while ago by a 'usually well-informed source' (a television cameraman — they don't miss anything!) that on a popular gardening programme with which he had been involved, one of the small army of researchers was allocated the specific task of standing close to a certain presenter while filming was under way. This researcher was most unusual among gardening programme staff in having a horticultural qualification and his role was to pay close attention to what the presenter said and did and make sure she didn't 'put her foot in it'.

I am happy to concede that there have been some remarkable and innovative gardeners and garden designers in the past who achieved much without formal training: Vita Sackville-West, Gertrude Jekyll, Lawrence Johnston to name just three of the most outstanding gardening names of the twentieth century. But they achieved what they did piecemeal; recognition came relatively late in life after the evidence of their abilities had become apparent. And they were always modestly aware of their own imperfections, most especially when it came to guiding others. Vita Sackville-West said of her articles in *The Observer*, 'I quailed at their incompleteness, their repetitiveness...'. You can't imagine Vita, for all her self-evident horticultural skills and abilities, presuming to front a gardening programme. Anyway, the gaunt, ungainly, unfeminine and scarcely attractive Miss Sackville-West wouldn't have a chance, not today, not in this country, because she wouldn't be a celebrity. In Tony Blair's media-mad Britain, you are nothing if you aren't a celebrity. What you need, as I have said on a previous occasion, is a pleasing appearance and good teeth and if you can't achieve celebrity status by being skilful at something, no matter, someone will create it for you. Would the Olympic sprinter Linford Christie have found his way onto a BBC list of television gardening presenters twenty years ago, as he is now? I can imagine Percy or Arthur or Clay having something colourful to say if he had.

Because of my rather well-publicised dissatisfaction

anne roper.

with some of the recent crop of gardening programmes, I have been accused of not wanting people to enjoy gardening or even of not finding the subject entertaining. Nothing could be further from the truth. I have always said a highly developed sense of humour is essential to garden in our climate and during my many years on *Gardeners' Question Time*, the natural humour and interplay between members of the panel as they swapped expertise and opinion was always one of its most marked and endearing features. But the humour was genuine, unforced and natural, not contrived. And in truth, I really don't have a quibble with gardening being used on television as an entertainment medium, just as cookery is with *Can't Cook, Won't Cook* and fashion with *What not to Wear*. My complaint is that these entertainment programmes weren't broadcast in addition to the real thing; they took its place.

I'm sometimes told that while *Ground Force* and the like didn't pretend to be serious horticulture, they were valuable because they encouraged people who would otherwise never even consider the subject to take their first gardening steps. Perhaps, and it's certainly fair to look at what the recent crop of programmes have achieved. They might have encouraged a growth in garden visiting although the highly efficient commercial activities of the Royal Horticultural Society, National Trust and the *Yellow Book* scheme have done more. Arguably they may have encouraged the sale of peat-free growing media in the cause of conserving peatlands and peat resources; although I'm sure this has in reality happened more through manufacturers offering these media to the exclusion of other options than by the public using informed discernment in making their choice. Similarly, they may have encouraged the more widespread appreciation of organic gardening; although I suspect this too is far more because gardeners now have immeasurably less choice. It is European legislation on chemicals that has driven forward organic gardening, not the message from our television screens.

The programmes may serve as a conduit for bringing to the public's notice new and commercially (if not necessarily horticulturally) worthy plant varieties. They certainly highlight new pieces of gardening equipment or gadgetry and they act as unpaid public relations outlets for commercial interests. But have they encouraged the growing of the most valuable and interesting varieties? Have they taught and helped perpetuate horticultura skills? Have they enhanced that great British strength and depth of gardening knowledge? I really don't think so. They seemed to fill a niche and a need, but in reality merely encouraged an essentially non-gardening audience to want more of the same. I think they can be compared with the radio station Classic FM which, I suspect, doesn't encourage more people to go to classical music concerts but probably does encourage them to listen to more of Classic FM.

Nonetheless, even if *Planet Patio* and its kind really have encouraged some people to take their first gardening steps, where has been the guiding hand to help them further? Above all it should be on the 'flagship', *Gardeners' World*. Sadly, however, it has lost its authority, in part because of the standard of the presentation but also because of the overall lack of credibility stemming from the location itself. It is divorced from the presenters' own gardens. From Percy Thrower at the Magnolias, through Arthur Billitt at Clacks Farm, Geoff Hamilton at Barnsdale and even Alan Titchmarsh at his hillside plot in Hampshire, the gardeners of the past presented the programme from their own gardens; although the slope was becoming both metaphorically and literally slippery by the time we reached Alan, who was clearly limited in what he could do by appearing to have no real kitchen garden and no real lawn.

Today, there's not even a pretence at ownership. The garden in Stratford-upon-Avon used for the programme is an anonymous plot miles from where the presenters live. They are bussed in on filming days, and don't and can't possibly relate to it any more than the viewers can. No-one seems to belong there. To identify with a garden, you need to see it and feel it, day in and day out through the seasons, experiencing its moods and moments. You need to wake up to the frosted leeks, see the morning sun rise over the dew-sodden lawn and realise it will be too wet to mow before midday, know what it means to have to put fleece over the tender seedlings last thing at night in late May, pause to regret not having sowed a carrot fly resistant variety and wonder why the apples have more codling moth in them this year than last. You should, quite simply, garden your own garden and that is where you should make your programmes. Then and only then can you convey real feeling and empathy to your viewers.

Sadly, I don't see much indication of any improvement in the near future. The gardening output overall is down, and when I spoke recently to a television commissioning editor and pleaded for at least some programmes that genuinely gave gardening help and instruction, he said that at present he only wanted 'design-based subjects'.

And thereby lies another sad tale; but that's for another day...

Pied Flycatcher

HAZEL CAVENDISH

Hunting wild turkeys

TIRED AND JET-LAGGED FROM A TRANSATLANTIC FLIGHT, I was being driven along US Route 10 South Highway on my way to a shooting lodge in the Catskill Mountains when I had my first sighting of them. A line of small dark brown fowl with long necks was scuttling at remarkable speed along the grass verge.

'What sort of game birds are those?' I asked, as they plunged into a thicket to escape our slip-stream. 'American wild turkey poults', said my host. 'Two hundred years ago the indigenous turkey was nearly extinct. Now there are said to be around four million of them which inhabit almost every state in the US except Alaska. You can see them in forest, field and even on suburban pavements in spring and autumn.'

Turkeys were widespread when the first Europeans arrived in America and occupied much of what is currently New York State, south of the Adirondack Mountains. Early settlers expanded westward and native forests were cleared, either to create arable land for agriculture or to obtain wood for fuel, and much valuable turkey habitat was lost. Turkeys were a useful source of fresh meat for hungry settlers.

As time went by the demand for wild turkey increased, and hunters began to sell available birds to markets in distant cities. Few birds were harvested. There were no hunting licences, nor were hunting seasons observed. By the mid-1800s the combination of habitat destruction and market hunting led to the catastrophic loss of New York State's original wild turkey population.

Fortunately, by the late 1940s, wild turkeys had expanded from a remnant population in northern Pennsylvania into south western New York State, and in 1957 a move to restore them to the rest of the state experienced phenomenal success. In the next thirty years, numbers increased from about 2,000 birds to over 65,000. Flocks of turkeys moved into the rugged Adirondack Mountains and the intensively-farmed Lake Plains region, and even to the suburbs of major cities.

Americans do nothing by halves when they decide to save a species for posterity. There are now five subspecies of wild turkey native to the US, each with its own environmental preferences. In 1990-3 rocket-propelled nets were used to trap hens from winter flocks in the towns of Pitcher, Pharsalia, Plymouth and Cincinnatus, and they were moved to other areas. The study focussed on hens because of their potential for reproduction. In another case, scientists experimented by fitting a transmitter to the back of each hen being moved, like a hiker wearing a backpack. Each transmitter weighed just over three ounces (80 g). After tagging, birds were released individually at the capture site. Most hens nested within five miles (8 km) of that town. The most extreme movement recorded was by a 'juvenile' hen which travelled almost thirty-five miles (55 km) in two weeks — proving that even in birds teenagers can be unpredictable!

Today's wild turkey population is highly successful, but the chief threats to breeding are posed by weather and predators. Poults suffer most from a wet winter and spring, but can cope with a normal winter's snow as long as their food supply holds up. Wild turkeys have been called 'vacuums of the forest' because of their varied food habits. Almost any item that has some nutritional value and can fit down a turkey's throat will be eaten.

The odds that a wild turkey nest will produce young are low because eggs and young chicks are popular food for ground-based predators, and hens nest on the ground. Racoons, skunks, mink, opossums, foxes, coyotes and black snakes all pose danger. In New York University's recent Wild Turkey Study, more than sixty per cent of 232 nests monitored did not produce any poults — but hens are obviously made of stern stuff. Most will try and nest again if it is not too late in the season, and the hen is in good physical condition.

The American wild turkey is a magnificent bird but differs in colour and shape from the plump professionally-produced bird which graces the British Christmas table.

The wild male (called a 'tom' or 'gobbler') has a dark black-brown body with metallic iridescence. During the strut display he has red, blue and white colours on his head, with caruncles and wattling on neck and chin — and a long 'beard', a tuft of continuously-growing bristle-like feathers jutting out from his chest. (This is not a totally reliable criterion for determining sex, however, because approximately five per cent of hens also have beards.) The female is rusty-brown with blue-grey head. Adult hens and toms weigh about 10-12 lbs (4.5-5.5 kg) in spring, rising to 16-20 lbs (7-9 kg) in late autumn. From a distance a wild turkey on the ground looks streamlined, with a sleek body, long pointed tail and slender legs, long neck and a narrow, relatively small wedge-like head.

Keen as they may appear to be on conservation of wildlife, the American countryman has turkey-hunting in mind when welcoming the success of their rising numbers.

Fortunately, wild turkeys are now legally protected as a game species in New York State, with spring and autumn hunting seasons. The spring season in May has regulations to protect the hens; October's fall season ends in mid-November and permits both hens and toms to be taken.

The autumn season bag limit varies with different regions. Legal hunting causes only about four per cent of the yearly mortality rate of adult hens, although the eight per cent from illegal poaching causes concern and is countered by a 'Turn-in-a-Poacher' hotline — where anyone can earn $100 if their tip leads to a poacher's conviction.

Turkey hunting should prove an all-American experience to the visitor from Britain or Europe. 'It can be exciting and memorable, but has associated dangers that the hunter must keep in mind', warns the National Wild Turkey Federation. Hunters need to wear camouflage as the turkey has keen sight — ten times the resolve power of a human with 270° peripheral vision — and easily detects colours or movement that are out of place in its woodland home. Their hearing is four times greater than that of a human, with an uncanny ability to pinpoint location of noise.

'Unfortunately camouflage not only reduces the turkey's chance of seeing the hunter, but has the same effect on hunters', warns the federation, 'Each year hunters are mistaken for turkeys and are shot. Hunters who choose to wear turkey colours — red, white, blue and black — are involved in a high proportion of accidents.' Friendly fire is not only a hazard in wartime, it would seem.

A visitor who expects to stalk his prey will be disappointed. Stalking is firmly discouraged. He has to position himself with his back to a tree 'large enough to break up your human outline while protecting your back from unsafe and unethical hunters who may try to sneak in on you, and shoot the turkey you are calling — or shoot at you'.

The instructions are: 'Don't stalk the gobbler — call it to you.' (The novice hunter is expected to know the right calls to persuade the gobbler that he is approaching a desirable female turkey, a call which the visitor is expected to have learnt from a summer foray in the woods beforehand. ('Pre-season scouting is important'.)

But what are the appropriate calls? 'Several soft tree yelps or clucks are generally enough — just enough to let the gobbler know a hen is nearby.'

If the visitor can manage to learn those calls in time for his day's hunting, help is at hand. There are many effective turkey calls on the market — box calls, slate calls, plush button calls, and diaphragm calls which are placed in the mouth. There is even a gobbler call. 'But don't use this one without actually hunting — you don't want to imitate the bird everyone is trying to shoot.'

'If another hunter does approach your position', says the National Wild Turkey Federation, 'remain still and call out to him in a loud voice. Do not wave or turkey — call to get another hunter's attention.'

Once the turkey flies down from his roost, a hunter can again start calling, but he is told to remember that calling too loudly or too frequently can cause the gobbler to become suspicious and 'hang up'.

His turkey may continue to gobble and display from the same spot and come no closer. To avoid this, the hunter must call 'just enough' to keep him coming. 'Muffle your calls so as to give the impression that the hen is moving away. If the gobbler goes silent, you never know for sure if he has left, or if he is coming in silently, looking for that stubborn hen that wouldn't come to him.'

(Any intrepid visitor to the United States who wishes to join a turkey hunt in New York State requires a turkey permit and one of the following licences: small game, sportsman, junior hunting, non-resident hunting or non-resident combination licence.)

Fly Agaric   Ink Caps

CALVIN JONES

Beach life is no picnic

ONE OF THE GREAT THINGS ABOUT LIVING ON AN ISLAND IS THE accessibility of our coastline. According to the Ordnance Survey, Britain has more than 11,000 miles (176,000 km) of it, and nobody lives more than seventy miles (110 km) from the sea.

It is little wonder that so many of us harbour fond memories of the seaside and that visiting the beach is essential for some once the weather starts to improve. But while we are enjoying the sunshine and sea air, beneath our feet the beach's permanent residents are busy going about their lives. For them the beach is anything but relaxing.

Take a close look at a handful of sand, and you will notice it is made up of many different types and sizes of particle. The main constituent of the sand around the coastline of the British Isles is silica fragments with some silt, clay and substances like shell fragments, diatoms and calcareous algae mixed in. The relative size and composition of the sand grains has a strong impact on the type, diversity and density of life that a beach can support.

Waves also have a great influence on the make-up of a beach as they pound against the shore. This wave action is the primary factor that determines the stability of the sand, the size of the grains deposited there, the beach's gradient, its drainage properties, its oxygen availability and its organic content.

In general the more exposed the beach the more pronounced the effects of the wave action, resulting in correspondingly coarser and less stable sand, a steeper gradient to the beach and less organic material — but that oversimplifies things. The consistency of the sand also varies both up and down a beach and along its length. Factors such as the wavelength and height of different wave types as they converge along the shore, the angle at which they strike, the shape and composition of the seabed and the influence of adjacent land-masses all have an impact on the make-up of a beach.

Add to this the twice-daily fluctuations introduced by the ebb and flow of every tide, and three different groups of predators (land predators, like waders and other birds, that come in to feed when the tide is out; marine predators, like fish, that come in with the tide; and of course the constant threat of predators living in the sand itself), and you begin to see that life beside the seaside is no picnic.

Because the wind and waves are constantly shifting the surface layer of sand, beaches offer scant purchase to would-be colonisers. The surface layer of the beach is also exposed to extreme fluctuations in temperature, salinity and to the drying effects of the sun and the wind when the

tide is out. The only really viable option is to burrow under the surface where conditions, while still difficult, are at least a little more stable.

A phenomenon known as capillary action draws water up into the tiny spaces between the grains of sand and serves to keep water levels under the beach significantly higher than sea level. Sheltered beaches in particular, with their smaller sand grains, tend to have better water-retaining properties than more exposed ones, and also contain more organic matter, a recipe that provides ideal conditions for a surprising array of life.

Plants generally do not like beaches. Rocks or large stones embedded in the sand can offer stable enough anchors for seaweed like the sea bootlace (*Chorda filum*) to take hold. This in turn offers a foothold for other species, like the epiphytic *Litosiphon pusillus*, which grows directly on the fronds of the larger algae.

During very low tides on sheltered shores, beds of eel-grass (*Zostera marina*) are sometimes exposed, while high on the beach, terrestrial plants like the dune-forming marram grass (*Ammophilia arenaria*), the sand sedge (*Carex arenaria*) and the sea mayweed (*Tripleurospermum maritimum*) are found.

Out on the sand itself the constantly moving surface tends to keep larger plants at bay, and microscopic algae living in the water-filled spaces between the sand grains are the only marine plants to occupy the beach itself. Microscopic animals also inhabit these tiny pockets of water. They tend to be flattened or threadlike forms, and include some of the smallest known species from most invertebrate groups. These minuscule beach dwellers often exist in huge numbers, but go largely unnoticed because of their small size.

Around the strand line it is common to find sand hoppers like *Talitrus saltator* and *Orchestia gammarella*. If disturbed, these small crustaceans propel themselves remarkable distances with an energetic flick of their specially adapted tails. Living so high on the shore, these creatures are immersed in seawater relatively infrequently, and have therefore evolved a way of extracting oxygen from the air. They emerge from shallow burrows at night to scavenge among the rotting weed left behind by the tide.

Out on the open beach, things look pretty barren at first, but closer inspection will usually reveal signs of a thriving community underfoot. Tiny tracks, holes or

depressions in the sand, casts, water spurts and small protruding tubes all betray the presence of buried creatures.

Burrowing is practically compulsory here, and it is hardly surprising that worms figure prominently. On more sheltered shores the ragworm *Nereis diversicolour* is abundant from the mid-shore down. These fast-moving, free-living worms are active hunters and use their strong, pincer-like jaws to catch and grip other worms, small crustaceans and just about anything else they can seize. They are sometimes seen crawling on the sand's surface, but usually burrow in search of their prey.

In contrast the lugworm (*Arenicola marina*), which is responsible for the familiar spaghetti-like casts on the lower shore, leads a relatively sedentary life. It is a sediment feeder that lives in a permanent U-shaped burrow. The head end of the 'U' is full of sand. When submerged

the worm actively pumps water through the burrow from the tail end forward across its gills to replenish its oxygen supply. The water is forced through the sand at the head end of the burrow, which effectively serves as a filter and traps any food particles suspended in the water. The worm then ingests the sand and digests the edible matter before voiding the indigestible sand as a cast at the tail end of the burrow.

Several species of worm found on our shores build protective tubes to live in. A narrow tube of sand protruding from the beach on the lower shore and sporting a fringe of sandy branches is likely to be the home of the sand mason (*Lanice conchilega*). The fringe of branches serves to protect the delicate tentacles that the worm uses to collect food when submerged. Although you only ever see about 1.6 inches (4 cm) of the tube sticking up out of the sand, it can be anything up to 12 inches (30 cm) long.

Molluscs — particularly bivalves — are also well represented on our sandy shores. Bivalves have two flattened shells (or valves) held together by a hinge-like ligament.

The group includes familiar edible species like mussels, cockles, oysters and scallops. Burrowing bivalves use their powerful muscular foot to loosen the sand, anchor themselves and pull themselves below the surface.

They are predominantly filter feeders, and when buried under the sand need access to the seawater above both to feed and to replenish their oxygen supply. They do this by extending two tube-like siphons to the surface of the sand — one to draw water in (the inhalant siphon), and one to let water back out (the exhalant siphon).

The common cockle (*Cerastoderma edule*) is a burrowing bivalve that lives buried 2 to 3 cm below the surface of the sand. It is often collected and, after filtering in clean seawater for a few hours, can be eaten. Another unmistakeable bivalve is the curved razorshell (*Ensis ensis*) which is forced to venture close to the surface of the sand to feed because of its short, fused siphon. The razorshell compensates for this forced proximity to the surface with a remarkable burrowing ability that allows it to disappear deep into the sand at the first sign of trouble. This speed-burrowing makes it difficult to unearth live specimens, but the presence of this unmistakeable bivalve is often betrayed by empty shells washed up on the beach.

Crustaceans of the sandy shore include the sand-hoppers already mentioned and sand-shrimps (*Gammarus spp*) often found under stones low on the shore. Opposum shrimps, or mysids, like the ghost shrimp (*Schistomysis spiritus*), are small, transparent shrimp-like crustaceans found at the edge of the sea or in pools left behind by the receding tide. The edible shrimp (*Crangon crangon*) is also found here, where it lies buried in the sand by day with only the tips of its antennae visible.

The shore crab (*Carcinus maenas*) is the most widespread crab on any British shore, including the beach. When the tide is out it burrows under the sand, emerging once submerged to scavenge for carrion, although it will take live prey if the opportunity presents itself. Lacking the protective carapace of its more familiar relative, the common hermit crab (*Pagurus bernhardus*) takes up residence in an empty mollusc shell for protection, moving into progressively larger accommodation as it grows. Sometimes found on the sand of the lower shore or in sandy pools, it is frequently joined in its shell by the small ragworm *Nereis fucata*, while both the anemone *Calliactis parasitica* and the hydroid *Hydractinea echinata*

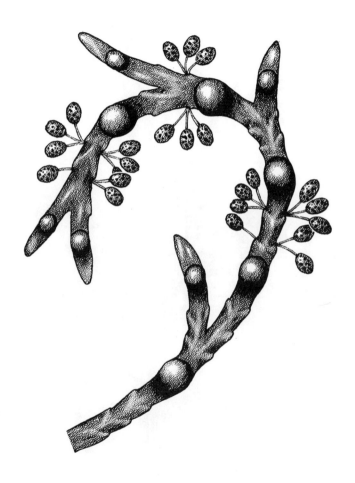

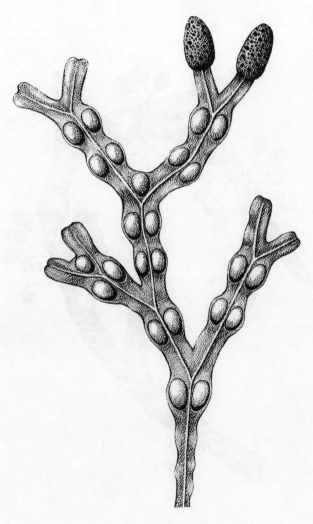

sometimes hitch a free ride on the outside of the shell. Crabs are messy eaters and these hitch-hikers benefit from scraps of food whenever the crab feeds.

A slight imprint in the sand close to low water may betray the presence of the sand star or burrowing starfish (*Astropecten irregularis*), which lives buried just below the surface. It feeds on worms, bivalves and crabs, swallowing them whole and ejecting the indigestible parts some time later. Another echinoderm, the sand brittlestar, is easily recognised with its distinct central disc and five long arms. It leaves a mark like a bird's foot on the surface of the sand where it lies buried just below the surface low on the shore. Sea urchins are also represented here: heart urchins are heart-shaped with soft, backward-pointing spines in place of the erect, rigid spines of their rocky-shore counterparts. They live buried up to four inches (10 cm) deep in the sand of the lower shore.

Sea anemones are perhaps among the last creatures you would expect to find buried in the sand, but there are some burrowing species, two of which, *Peachia hastata* and *Halcampa chrysanthellum*, occasionally occur at low water on very sheltered shores.

As well as providing a permanent home for residents, beaches are an important resource for visiting species. They offer sheltered, food-rich nursery grounds for many flatfish species, including plaice (*Pleuronectes platessa*), flounder (*Platichthys flesus*) and sole (*Solea solea*). Small flatfish are common near the water's edge and in sandy pools.

Wading birds take advantage of the wealth of invertebrate life on offer and regularly fly in to feed on the rich pickings. Along with estuarine mudflats, British beaches form a vital network of feeding grounds for many migratory bird species.

Rocky shore animals like the edible mussel (*Mytilus edulis*) and the acorn barnacle (*Semibalanus balanoides*) often blanket rocks on the periphery of sandy shores, and familiar seaweed like wracks (*Fucus spp*) and kelps (*Laminaria spp*) quickly take hold wherever conditions are suitable. These colonisers in turn attract other species to settle and it is not uncommon to find thriving rocky shore communities alongside, and occasionally right in the middle of a sandy beach.

While beaches may not immediately spring to mind when we think of coastal wildlife, they are far from the barren expanses of sand they can at first appear to be. So the next time you are sitting on a beach and grow weary of basking in the oh-so-fickle British sunshine, get up and explore. You might be surprised by what you find.

References:

Barnes, R D, *Invertebrate Zoology* (fifth edition 1987), CBS College Publishing, Philadelphia.

Barrett, J, and Yonge, C M, *Collins Pocket Guide to the Sea Shore* (1958), Collins, London.

Challinor, H, Murphy-Wickens, S, Clark, J, & Murphy, A, *A Beginner's Guide to Ireland's Seashore* (1999), Sherkin Island Marine Station, Sherking Island, Co Cork.

Fitter, R, and Ray, S, *Collins Gem Guide — The Seashore* (1984), Collins, London.

Press, J R, Sutton, D A, & Tebbs, B M, *Reader's Digest Nature Lover's Library — Field Guide to the Wild Flowers of Britain* (1981), Reader's Digest Association Limited, London.

Tait, R V, *Elements of Marine Ecology — an introductory course*, (third edition 1981), Butterworths, London.

Websites:

UK Marine Special Areas of Conservation: www.ukmarinesac.org.uk/index.htm.

'Atlantic Sandy Shores and Dunes', eNature.com: www.enature.com/habitats/show_lifezone.asp?lifezoneID=13 —,.

'Marine Biotopes of Britain and Ireland', Sligo Institute of Technology: www.itsligo.ie/biomar/INDEX.HTM.

BILL TAYLOR

Sweet taste of success

AS THE SELF-PROCLAIMED AND UNPAID INTERNATIONAL ambassador for Loupiac wines, Alain Forment has a simple marketing strategy. He puts a few bottles of Loupiac in his suitcase wherever he travels, and spreads the word and the taste at every opportunity. In the late 1970s, it paid off handsomely when one of Japan's biggest corporations sent the company's jumbo jet to Bordeaux to clean up all the available stocks of this luscious sweet wine. For the most part, though, Alain's enthusiasm can never be a match for the marketing big guns of New World wines.

Bordeaux has had a few troubled years. While the superstars of the Médoc, St Emilion and Pomerol revel in their best vintages for a decade, and put up prices to match, French wine sales are collapsing in the face of intense competition from the New World, especially Australia and Chile.

A few years ago, French wine exports to Britain — traditionally its best market — had fallen by nearly a fifth, and sales to Germany were down almost as much. Wine and spirit exports are worth nearly £5 billion a year to the French economy, so the problem is serious. One Bordeaux merchant has talked of potential 'catastrophe' unless drastic changes are made soon.

Whatever the mystique and kudos surrounding wine making, vineyard owners are fundamentally small farmers. They share the passions, prejudices and bad jokes of small farmers all over the world. (How do you make a small fortune from your vineyard? Start with a large one!) The Loupiac growers are interesting as individuals and as a group because they believe fervently that small, artisanal producers make wonderful wines — and to prove the point, they are willing to go to war with the enormously powerful corporate interests of the global wine brands.

The battle lines in this commercial war are clearly drawn. Bordeaux is accused of arrogance, outrageous prices and a patrician indifference to the desires of the vast majority of ordinary wine drinkers. The New World is aggressively focussed on the market place.

'Our attitude is to make wines people want to drink as opposed to wines winemakers want to make', says Terry Davis, the managing director of the Californian-Australian conglomorate Beringer Blass. 'We put sunshine in a bottle, fruit-driven wines you don't have to put down for ten years.'

And according to Giancarlo Bianchetti of the Chilean winemakers Concha y Toro: 'Knowledgeable consumers know France and the best French wines, but maybe the mass market finds them a bit snobbish. Tradition is not necessarily an advantage. It depends how you manage it.'

Ironically, Bordeaux's salvation may lie not with the great chateaux, who will always have a market for their wines, but with the little people. Luxury wines account for less than five per cent of the output of the region, and a little humility might go a very long way with consumers outside France.

Loupiac is the smallest *appellation controllée* in Bordeaux, making unfortified sweet white wines like Sauternes across the river, but at half the price in the shops. The growers want to expand sales to Britain, but have no marketing budget or staff, apart from the peripatetic and unpaid Alain Forment. One of the growers is also an enthusiastic private pilot, and will jump in his small plane to visit a potential customer if he feels the message is not getting through.

To make any inroads into the UK, they will have to change the tastes of a generation of British drinkers, persuading them that chilled sweet wine is delicious not only as a dessert wine, but as an aperitif, with cheese, with foie gras and with some meats that have spicy or sweet-ish sauces. (Try chilled Loupiac with blue cheese on toast as a starter at dinner.)

The growers run big risks in the vineyard. The grapes are picked after the onset of noble rot, where the natural fungus *Botrytis cinerea* attacks ripe grapes, extracting moisture and leaving a natural balance of intense sweetness and acidity. At the *vendage*, they not only pick the grapes by hand, but grape by grape, going over the harvest several times to make sure the raw materials of the wine are as near perfect as possible.

Many proprietors also make red and dry white wine as

a banker against crop failure, but Loupiac is their love affair. 'It's difficult, and every year it's different', says Michel Boyer at Château du Cros. 'Why do I do it? Well, it's in my family, which is the tradition, but it's mainly in my heart. It is my passion.'

These men and women number themselves among the artisans of the wine world, proud to identify with special-ist cheesemakers or Parma ham producers. They work with their own hands in their own vineyards most days of the year, light years away from the absentee corporate land-lords of some of the great chateaux. And they are to New World wines what the Slow Food Movement is to McDonalds.

Not surprisingly, the vignerons of Loupiac think their artisanal approach is one way to take on New World wines, where consistency and mass market appeal are the watchwords. But the Loupiac growers are none too impressed with the support they're getting from the chiefs of the Bordeaux wine trade.

'A small *appellation controllée* like Loupiac faces an enormous struggle to get its message across', says Didier Sanfourche, of the highly regarded Château Loupiac-Gaudiet. 'This is Bordeaux, too, but hardly anyone outside France has ever heard of us. We do happen to sell well in Wakefield, but that's only because the man from the local supermarket was passing through and paid us a visit and fell in love with our wines.'

At a Saturday evening gathering of Loupiac growers and their wives, where everyone tucked into enormous cuts of steak Bordelaise barbecued on a vinewood fire, one grower was much less restrained after a few glasses of very fine claret.

'Ask the big men up in town why everyone thinks Bordeaux is so snooty? The answer is there are two Bordeaux, the Grand Crus and everyone else. The big chateau will always be OK. It's time we did more for the little boys.'

Well, Eric Dulong is one of the big men of Bordeaux, head of the organisation that represents all the region's wine trade. And he freely acknowledges there's a problem.

'Bordeaux has too much the image of being only for rich people with a good knowledge of wine. But I am also concerned about the ninety-five per cent of Bordeaux wines that are non-luxury wines and need a lot of help. It's partly an image thing. When you're at the top, people want to knock you off your pedestal. We need to spend a lot telling our growers how to compete with the New

World. If we don't change now, we will suffer in a few years. Indeed, the next five to ten years will be very difficult for French wines.'

As he spoke, Steve Daniel of Oddbins was travelling throughout the south-west of France looking for new growers and new wines. He's on the side of Loupiac.

'Bordeaux gives the impression of being very high-brow. Many customers feel daunted by French wines, and if you don't know what you're doing there are great risks involved. With Australian wines you always know what you're going to get. Often that's a good thing, but some-times it's very boring. Here in Bordeaux, there are a lot of nice little producers and maybe they should be given a chance to shine.'

Back in Loupiac, it's the one day of the year when tra-dition is given pride of place. The annual gala of the Guild of Loupiac Winemakers has a deliberately medieval touch with velvet cloaks and very fine hats and a solemn cere-mony to 'knight' new friends. At the party afterwards, members of a circus troupe tease the guild leaders and knock some hats off, literally and metaphorically. It's a deliberate attempt by the growers to be true to their tradi-tions, but also to present an unstuffy image to the outside world.

'That could never happen in Margaux', said one grower with a smile.

COLIN BECKINGHAM

Sugar shack mountain

I RECALL QUITE CLEARLY THOSE YOUTHFUL RAMBLES: THE BOYISH
sprint to the top of St Catherine's Hill near Winchester
that ended breathlessly about halfway up; footing the
maze cut into the chalk turf towards the grove of old
beeches at the summit; long strolls along the banks of the
Itchen imagining the barges of days long gone by; summer days at Farley Mount; and Dorset dawdles, uncover-
ing curious historic milestones apparently miles from any
modern road while chasing down Hardy's scenic characters. From my fireside here in the Canadian woods these
distant memories, once so familiar, seem oddly foreign —
the Canadian rambling experience is so different.

We should note that, to many Canadians, a 'rambler' is
someone whose thoughts are expressed aimlessly and dis-
connectedly. People who like walking for its own sake are
hikers. And hiker interests tend to be quite closely related
to other activities like canoeing, backpacking and cross-
country skiing for reasons we shall see a bit later.

Australia has echoes of the rambling spirit in the notion of going walkabout, but it rings slightly oddly in the historic North American context, where walking for its own sake was not very productive. Travelling long distances on foot or horseback was something one did of necessity, and the original roads were the rivers, since they afforded the most effective way of getting about.

The Canadian countryman's calendar begins in the cold of the winter. This is a cold that the British rambler would not know. There is also heat and prolonged sunshine, but recent experience in the United Kingdom with such meteorological extremes means that British ramblers are all too familiar with this. However, the cold, and by this I mean extremes of cold down to -35° Celsius (not including windchill) overnight, is another matter. You cannot afford to be caught with insufficient clothing or food; the consequences can be deadly.

So we learn to dress on the side of caution and carry reserves of food, and ensure that we know where we are going. I see quite a difference between being disoriented in the openness of Dartmoor or the North York Moors and the same experience in the depths of a Canadian thicket. Without the long distance landmarks of an open space or a global positioning system, the sun and a cool head become the only assets at hand.

There are winter skills to learn, and crossing frozen water is a particularly exciting one. When the ice is thick the path is secure, offering views from the centre of a lake that you could not otherwise enjoy without a boat. Skating on thin ice can lead to very difficult moments. Depth of snow, often amounting to three feet (1 m) or more in the shelter of the forest, means that walking is no longer practical, so we use snowshoes or skis.

March arrives and the moderating temperatures, fluctuating above and below freezing, squeeze the maples like sponges and they begin to yield their sap. Drill a hole in the tree and sweet water drips out. Trudging from tree to tree with buckets of collected sap to be boiled at the campfire means that a countryman does quite enough walking in and around his own bush without yearning for walking for its own sake. Carrying buckets of sap back to the collection point is a very warming occupation, and it is particularly amusing for bystanders when you slip in the wet snow and dump the collected sap into your boots.

The sugar shack is a uniquely North American feature of the country. Take a simple allotment shed, put a wood stove inside, add some vents to the roof to allow steam to escape, invite a few friends along to sit on bolts of firewood and watch the syrup evaporate and thicken, test the product as it progresses, start telling tall stories and you have a place where H E Bates' Uncle Silas would have fitted in very well.

The 'sugaring off' season comes to an end in April, by which time we can start thinking of walking for fun. The snow gets thinner and thinner, and the grass that was green last November emerges brown and exhausted. The sun is noticeably stronger, and the days longer. The ground is wet but passable.

But 'passable' is only a relative term. The ground has been frozen from just before Christmas to the end of March so the warm April showers that are supposed to bring forth May flowers hit the remains of the snow, causing it to melt rapidly. But the water cannot penetrate the ground because it is still frozen. The water immediately runs off at high speed to lower ground to the delight of the beavers but the dismay of the rambler who forgot to bring his canoe and needs either to make a major detour or go home.

The wetness goes on. With the warm sun the frost starts to come out of the ground. This huge block of ice is melting from the top down, so as it melts it cannot percolate through the still frozen layers, but sits on the surface making sure your boots are never dry.

Finally, things are dry enough to walk without squelching everywhere in wellies. Flowers begin to emerge. The familiar primrose and coltsfoot are nowhere to be seen; instead we have trillium, dog's-tooth violet and Dutchman's breeches. The pervading smell is one of damp, rotting leaves.

We can't wait to get out and about. But Canada has no real bridleway system. We do not see the familiar wooden signposts that punctuate the British countryside, the result of centuries of agricultural use and public passage. The sight of a stile is a very rare event. However, there are systems of marked trails open to walkers that have been established in recent years.

One that passes fairly close to my property is the Rideau Trail; the small orange triangles nailed to a tree or a fence post marking the way are visible from time to time where they cross a main highway. These marked trails connect large tracts of publicly owned land such as provincially and federally owned parks. The Rideau Trail in particular passes through a provincial wilderness park known as Frontenac Park, and it is in such wide-open spaces that the Canadian weekend rambler gets most of his country-side experience. Frontenac Park, small by Canadian standards, has more than 12,000 acres (5,000 ha) of wilderness, allowing the countryman to explore without confinement to a pathway.

The sections of the trail that are on private land were slowly established with the permission of the owners. One of the keys to maintaining their goodwill is to encourage users to stay to the permitted paths. There is an effort under way to form a trail that links one end of Canada to the other, but it is so far incomplete.

Tony Nicholls, a keen rambler formerly from Hampshire now living in Southwestern Ontario, tells of one of the longer trails:

'The Bruce Trail is Canada's oldest marked hiking trail. It was conceived in 1960 and completed in 1967, which is young compared to the UK. It is about 500 miles (800 km) long and has over 180 miles (300 km) of side trails. It follows the Niagara Escarpment from Niagara Falls to Tobermory on the Bruce peninsula on Lake Huron.'

Tony has hiked the complete length of this trail, in sections, over a number of years.

One of the reasons to ramble is to see wildlife in their varied habitats, wildlife that becomes more varied as the spring advances. Bears emerge from hibernation, birds return from their holiday in Mexico and the Caribbean, and cold-blooded reptiles emerge into the sun to warm on hard rocks. As Tony Nicholls recalls:

'The Massasauga Rattlesnake is Ontario's only poisonous snake, whose bite can kill a small child. One warm sunny midsummer day I was extremely lucky to see two of

them intertwined. As I tried to take a close-up photo I heard the threatening rattle and in my haste to retreat only managed to capture a blurred image of my finger — their privacy was protected!'

We catch sight of a shiny black creature the size of a large dog with a perfectly curved back galloping shallowly on stubby front legs — it is an otter; the basil brush leaping up and down on the spot trying to scare field voles from their grassy tunnels is the familiar fox, but might possibly be a lynx; the heavy furry thing twice the size of a large cat that crosses your path without a care in the world is a raccoon looking for trouble.

Often we see not the wildlife itself, but the destruction they leave behind. That damage twenty feet (6 m) up where the juicy bark has been stripped from a maple tree was caused by a brown ball that looks like a cuddly koala bear but in fact is a porcupine (a lorry-sized hedgehog) whose stiff and sharp quills will stick in your skin and itch painfully for days. The tree that is blocking your path probably was felled by a beaver who was either looking for food in the succulent upper branches or material to stuff up a gap in his latest dam. And that depression in the exposed sandy soil which looks as though it was swept untidily with a broom is where a snapping turtle dug a hole with her back legs to lay her eggs, which will likely be dug up and eaten by the fox a few days later.

In Hampshire, summer evenings would occasionally bring out the midges. Here insects operate at a different level of magnitude. First, the rambler who is looking forward to a spring walk in May after a long winter inside enters a patch of forest and is immediately surrounded by a cloud of small black biting insects that find every exposed patch of skin and start digging trenches for extended warfare. Favourite places are between the top of your ear and the brim of your hat, or behind the temple arms of your glasses. These wounds swell up and itch. Fortunately black flies are a nuisance only for a couple of weeks, but then the mosquitoes take over, causing more swellings and itching. Eventually the mosquitoes dry up in the long days of summer. But the arrival of heat just encourages the deer flies and horse flies that are the real harpies of the bush.

These guys are no joke. About the size of a housefly, they do not appear everywhere you ramble, but where they do they can bite hard. They are very strong fliers, and will keep up even if you run. The flies harass you while you are changing for a swim. As you swim underwater they cannot get you, but they hover patiently waiting for you to come up to breathe, at which time they bite any wet baldness they can find.

The calendar moves on and supplies of insect repellent run low; but by mid-August all three of these insect mercenaries have faded, having done their year's worth of mischief and caused sufficient misery. Then the rambler can go where he will and enjoy, largely unmolested, the remnants of the summer in perfect sunny bliss. Late summer and the autumn are the glory days of Canadian rambling.

At this time Canada smells of warm hay, hot rocks, basswood and sweet clover. Until, of course, you walk past the pig farm. There's nothing like the smell of freshly spread manure to put a spring in your step, inflate a pace to a pace and three-quarters and get that rucksack swinging on your back. In such cases it is nice to be mobile. There are increasingly cases in Canada of people who build houses in the country in search of peace and quiet, only to find that the normal operations of neighbourhood farms suddenly assault the nostrils for days on end. Complaints to the authorities are ineffective since the practice of muck spreading is a well-established part of country life.

Summer here does not bring my old friends, patches of bluebells or fields of gorse; there are other flowers such as

bergamot and goldenrod, but nothing as dramatic as the British sea of blue. Also the blackberry, so common on chalk downland and so welcome for snacks on a long ramble, is replaced in my area by the thimbleberry or black raspberry, which is smaller and less juicy but still quite sweet.

The summer declines, the leaves start falling, maple leaves turn to deep yellows and reds, the wild grapes mature, the geese start flying south, and rambling continues with thicker sweaters and stronger boots. Eastern Canada is not the 'Wild West' but we do see guns, which are an essential part of a countryman's life and business. In Britain it is not uncommon for a rambler to see a shotgun cradled in the arms of a gamekeeper as he tries to tell you how unhappy he is that you might be disturbing his feathered friends. You protest that you are on a pathway recognized since the inception of the enclosure system, but it makes no difference. In Canada the gun is more likely to be carried by a hunter, legally or illegally.

Controlled hunting is a recognized part of wildlife population control here during certain defined seasons mostly in the fall, and people are familiar with guns and their role in country life. Ramblers make it their business to know when and where they may be likely to run into parties of hunters, and if you go rambling in the hunting season then you talk in a loud voice or allow your frying pan to clang against the tin cup and saucepan as you boldly advance along the trail. As a result you do not see much wildlife, but at least hunters realise that turkeys and deer do not make a racket as they make their way through the bush. And of course the curses of the hunters add to the noise as they thank you for scaring away the game.

Illegal hunting is much more of a concern. As it comes to Christmas time, people may be tempted to test the limits of permission to hunt to get their Christmas dinner. The rambler thinks that hunting is over for the season, but nearby explosions soon indicate that for some people it is not. Time to make yourself obvious again.

And so, dear rambler, as you suffer the extended rain of a Dorset vale or the cloudy bluster of a Yorkshire Moor, reassure yourself that you have not fallen through thin ice to die slowly of hypothermia, you are not suffering the mosquitoes, black flies, and deer flies of the Canadian bush, and your rambling rights are firmly entrenched in history. The sun is probably shining over here, but the grass is not necessarily greener.

KATHERINE GOW

Doing it for themselves

ANOTHER COUNTRY, DIFFERENT PRIORITIES. OVER THE LAST SIX months, I have been hearing from women throughout India about their rural lives, and the daily struggle to make ends meet and create a more hopeful future for their children. By our standards, many of their stories are heartbreaking. I expected that. But at the same time, it is astonishing how often human ingenuity triumphs and creates bright solutions to problems that seem completely daunting.

One example is the poultry farm that has been transformed into a school in the village of Alur in Andhra Pradesh. This school is the cornerstone of a nationwide campaign to stop slave labour among children, especially girls. It is run by the Mamidipudi Venkatarangaiya Foundation (MVF), and in just over ten years the organisation has helped more than a quarter of a million children who otherwise would not have had any schooling at all.

Alur village is their first camp for girls. And in the simple whitewashed rooms where the girls stay, many of the children still cannot comprehend the advantages of education. But here they get a chance to be children again, in a world of lessons, fun and games. They don't do any work here — hired villagers do the cooking, cleaning and washing. This is a strategy to ensure that the children continue studying.

Mala Andalu arrived recently after labouring in cotton fields for some years. Her wages of thirty pence a day went to her parents. She worked long hours spraying pesticide on the crops. The chemicals left blisters on her hands, but when she skipped work because of the pain, she was scolded by her employers. She says simply that the school camp is better than home: 'Here we study; there we worked.' Her friend Paramjyoti, thirteen, had to drop out of school to take care of her brother's child. Today she is happy studying again and reveals shyly that her favourite subject is science.

These school camps often bring about a completely different outlook for the families as well as the children. The school head at Alur, Pakanati Vani, is like an elder sister to the girls. She has been working in MVF camps for five years and says that once parents are convinced of the value of education, they proudly visit their children with gifts and even bring cameras to take pictures. And the mothers readily take over the girls' work at home.

Many of the children were bonded labour. They were freed through dialogue with parents and employers, with the support of local groups and volunteers. Getting girls out of the cotton fields and into school was a big challenge. Farmers insisted that only young girls who had not reached puberty could pluck the cotton plants. They said the crop became 'unproductive' if touched by older girls, but this was merely an excuse to exploit cheap child labour.

Another issue that MVF has tackled uncompromisingly is child marriage. Gaganam Yadamma, thirteen, had never been to school but worked with the local school-child committee and was aware of the ills of an early marriage. When her widowed mother was pressurised to fix Yadamma's marriage, she informed local volunteers. Members of the village council spoke to the groom's parents, threatening them with legal action. The bride's family was fined and warned that all state benefits would be withdrawn if they persisted. The wedding was called off! Although villagers continue to perform child marriages, many girls see the MVF programme as a means of escaping early marriage.

Children who have never been to school lack confidence, so the MVF village camps became a halfway house to prepare children for regular school. Almost 100 per cent of the girls now go straight on to school from the camps.

At Alur, girls appear confident interacting with schoolteachers and literate peers. Laughter comes easily to them. Dressed neatly in colourful skirts, the pen tucked into their blouse is a symbol of their new life.

—

Education offers a whole new future for these children that would just not be possible if they remained trapped in subsistence agricultural labouring — albeit to help their poor families put food on the table. But school is only ever part of the story. A whole new breed of women with no formal education at all is helping to bring about a technological revolution in some of the poorest areas of rural India.

Gulab Devi is forty-five and lives in the village of Harmara in the Ajmer district of Rajasthan. She is the sole breadwinner for her four children and an ailing husband who has never had a job during the twenty-four years of their marriage. Gulab is also completely illiterate.

Ask her what she does for a living, and she'll tell you she makes electronic circuits and chargers for solar lighting panels. And before you start wondering whether you have heard her correctly, she'll tell you that she also installs and maintains hand pumps, water tanks and pipelines. Not only is she running her household comfortably with her salary from this work, she is also one of the most respected members of her community. Gulab is one of the many Barefoot Solar Engineers (BSEs) working across eight Indian states to establish solar energy systems in areas where electricity supply is either non-existent or highly erratic. A majority of these engineers, mostly women, are illiterate like Gulab or semi-literate at best. But they talk of transformers, coils and condensers like other Indian women would talk of cooking and sewing.

The Ministry of Non-Conventional Energy Sources, the European Commission and the United Nations Development Programme (UNDP) all support the Barefoot Solar Engineering programme. It is implemented by the Barefoot College, also known as the Social Work Research Centre, based in Rajasthan. Set up by noted social worker Bunker Roy, the Barefoot College addresses community problems by building upon people's skills and placing the solutions to their problems in their own hands.

'The focus is on sustainable use of solar energy. People should be able to do their own solar engineering according to their own needs', says Bhagwat Nandan Sewda, the focal person of the BSE programme.

Kausalya of Buharu village in Tilonia presents another graduate of the college. All of nineteen, Kausalya is adept at fixing and maintaining solar energy systems. What she is also good at is local governance. She used to attend the village night school when Barefoot College introduced the Bal Sansad, or the Children's Parliament. The concepts of local, state and central governments were explained to school students, who were encouraged to compete for the posts of legislators for the Bal Sansad. Prompted by other girls who were too timid to take on male students, Kausalya filed her nomination. She was the token candidate of the entire female electorate, and bagged the post from her school.

Then followed the prime ministerial contest in which all the legislators from over fifty schools in Tilonia contested. Once again she got all the girl votes, while some infighting among others got her a substantial chunk of the boy votes. Kausalya became the prime minister of the Bal Sansad at the age of thirteen. In three years of heading the Sansad, Kausalya's 'cabinet' solved a host of problems — from the lack of electricity in one village school to local land disputes.

Life took another turn when she came of age and was packed off to her husband's home (she had been married when just a few years old) in Jaipur's Pandwa village. Here too, Kausalya worked on the infrastructure of Pandwa, including solar lights and a new water pipeline. Unhappy with her 'activism' to begin with, her husband and parents-in-law gradually came to admire her efforts.

'My husband will never say it, but I know he's very proud of me', says Kausalya. 'Now he asks me to maintain his accounts for him.'

Barefoot's project partners are encouraged by the response to the programme, which has received the Stockholm Challenge Award for Environment in 2002.

'The project has empowered women. Illiterate and semi-literate women are operating and repairing energy systems. It has also freed them from the drudgery of searching for fuel-wood and reduced the health hazards of burning wood-fires', says Maurice Dewulf of the UN Development Programme. 'The project has demonstrated how solar energy provides a solution not just for cooking and lighting but also for education, agriculture, health, and income-generation.'

Another case in point is twenty-six-year-old Ritma Bharti from Bihar's West Champaran district. Her village Bahurva had no provision for electricity; sunset meant the end of all economic activity for the day, including her husband's shop. When she heard about the solar training workshop, she told her husband she wanted to go. Her husband agreed, although her mother-in-law threw a fit. But Ritma was adamant and took off for the six-month workshop, her two-year-old in tow.

By the end of the workshop, she had prepared eighty solar lanterns to carry back home. She installed these in forty schools in the area, and looked after their maintenance as well. Ritma has gradually trained many fellow villagers in the operation and repair of these lanterns, and more than 750 lanterns are now being used to run schools, irrigation facilities, shops and medical centres late into the evening.

What Ritma is personally happiest about is that women's self-help groups can use these lanterns to meet after sunset, as their daytime is packed with domestic chores. Each woman saves a fistful of foodgrain every day. At the end of the month, all the foodgrain is sold, and the money carefully put away for cheap lending to any member in times of need. This banking system has only been possible because of the nightly meetings of the group.

'I now look back at my childhood when I always dreamt of doing something big for my society', Ritma says. 'My mother used to laugh at me. Today my family, my neighbours, and even the village elders respect me and value my contributions. It feels wonderful.'

Similar stories are unfolding in the north-eastern parts of the country. Pretty, cheerful and enthusiastic Devi from Sikkim has been a solar engineer since the age of fifteen. She has helped establish solar panels in four districts of Sikkim, covering even the most remote areas. People are now using solar energy for heating, water supply, and running fax and STD systems. Devi looks back on the earlier days and laughs.

'When I first talked of solar training, the boys in the neighbourhood mocked me and said I would look ridiculous climbing poles to set up the panels. At that time I was too timid to retort. Now my work speaks for itself, and even the boys come to me for advice on various matters. I have even started joining them in their football games!'

Little things mean a lot, as the song says. Perhaps we do too little with the enormous resources we have.

Footnote: with thanks to Shruti Gupta, Sarika Jain Antony and the Women's Feature Service of India.

MATTHEW HOLT

Two men in a boat

THE RIVER THAMES, THE AORTA OF ENGLAND. STARTING AS A slender stream in the Cotswolds, it gently meanders through the pastures of middle England picking up tributaries and pace, till it reaches the capital, powerful and wide, and then disappears into the grey anonymity of the North Sea. England's tumultuous history has been acted out along its banks. And it has been a silent muse for generations of poets and writers. 'Sweet Thames, run softly, till I end my song'.

It was with such pretentious thoughts, and admittedly after a few drinks, that my friend JB and I decided to row the Thames. Or at least a manageable portion of it. After consulting the charts, we settled on the section from Oxford to Richmond, a journey of some ninety-five miles (150 km). As our guide we took Jerome K Jerome's *Three Men in a Boat*. Published in 1889, it describes how Jerome and his idling companions travel by skiff from Kingston to Oxford. In amongst a rambling commentary on the manners and mores of Victorian England is a reasonably detailed description of the route. We had only to hope that it had not changed too much in the intervening years.

Day One: Oxford to Abingdon

During an uncommonly hot English summer, we caught the train to Oxford and made our way to Donnington Bridge, where we took possession of our craft. The Wherry was awaiting us, tethered to the bank like an impatient race horse. It was a sleek, twenty-five-foot (7.5 m) double sculling skiff. It would be our carriage and home for the next six days. By suspending a canvas awning from metal struts we could transform it into a floating tent, and on removing the seats could stretch out not too uncomfortably head-to-toe. We stowed our belongings in the bow and clambered aboard. Then, with a hurried wave to the boat's owner, who watched anxiously from the bank, we were off.

Donnington Bridge is the start of the Oxford University eights rowing course. It seemed a propitious place to depart. Briefly. For we had no sooner pushed off, than eights' crews flashed past us like arrows. In reply we pulled mighty strokes of air and loudly clashed our blades. For initially it proved difficult to marry our differing styles. JB was, by his own admission, a college rower of some note, the sort who modestly displays an oar in his living room. Whereas I was a rawer talent, my experience limited to Sunday picnic trips from Richmond. However, we eventually managed to achieve a modicum of forward propulsion and began to lurch our way downriver.

At Iffley we successfully negotiated our first lock, stubbornly defying the lounging drinkers on the bank, who watched on willing a disaster. And at Sandford we sailed through our second lock with brio. Then we were free, rowing into the heart of England, passing through gentle

pastures and green fields, beneath Radley College's haughty gaze. The river was quiet and empty, the only noise the slap of oars and the creak of the bow, as we slid through the water.

After three hours, we had covered seven miles (12 km), which we considered a fair showing for our first day. So we stopped for the night at Abingdon, pulling into a quiet backwater opposite the Nags Head. But manoeuvring a twenty-five-foot skiff in close quarters is not an easy task. And for the next half-hour, to cries of encouragement from the pub's clientele, we bumped back and forth between the two banks, like learner drivers who have been given an articulated lorry to park. Jerome thought Abingdon 'a typical country town of the smallest order — quiet, eminently respectable, clean and desperately dull'. But he had evidently not been there for disco night at the Nags Head, nor encountered the enthusiastic pub band. We spent our first night under canvas on the river serenaded by murderous cover song renditions and whooping choruses.

Day Two: Abingdon to Moulsford

I awoke to find a pale, pink sun peeping through the light mist that hung on the river. As the sun rose, the water was set alight, like liquid fire. It was beautiful and made me keen to seize the day. But I then discovered that our vessel had shipped quite a lot of water during the night, and that most of my belongings were sodden. An hour later, after we had bailed the boat and wrung the water out of our clothes, we pulled out of Abingdon.

Come noon, we tied up on the bank and set off across the fields towards a distant church spire. Dorchester-upon-Thames: once a Roman fort and capital of Saxon Wessex, but these days just a quiet, dreamy village, fortunately well stocked with pubs.

After lunch, we were back on the river, heading south past Shillingford and Wallingford. By now we were coming to terms with our task and at times there was even a hint of coordination to our endeavour. There are two distinct roles involved in propelling a two-man skiff down the river: the Stroke and the Cox. The Stroke sits at the stern of the boat, or the rear. He is responsible for setting the rhythm and pace. He can perceive the boat's course from the trail of wake, but presumes that it reflects the shape of the river or obstacles ahead. Meanwhile, the Cox is seated at the bow, or the front. Glancing regularly over his shoulder, it is his task to set the course by putting more weight on one oar or the other. Only he is truly aware of the hopelessly erratic line they are pursuing as the boat corkscrews from

bank to bank. And the Stroke must have full confidence in the Cox's navigation. For if he starts adding his own touch to the steering, it becomes immensely complicated.

The process is not always perfect. I was stroking the boat, pulling hard, though noticing that the left-hand bank was getting uncomfortably close. However, I confidently presumed that JB, as cox, would rectify the line. But he didn't. And when I did finally glance over my shoulder, I just had time to see him curled up in a foetal position, before we ploughed deep into an overhanging gorse bush. Whereas JB thought the incident amusing and gave it no more thought, my faith in the whole arrangement was shaken. For the rest of the trip, my mind would suddenly conjure up images of huge cruise boats or bridge spans looming before us, causing me to spasmodically glance over my shoulder like a nervous twitch.

By early evening we reached Moulsford and elected to grace the Beetle and Wedge Inn with our patronage. But the intervening century had taken its toll on our guide-book. For what were once hearty, welcoming pubs for the river traveller, were now stiff-mannered, high-priced hostelries for City sorts. So, when we pulled alongside the tidy pontoon, attired in our sweat-stained rowing shorts, the French waiters did not rush to help us in. But to be fair, after a change of clothing, we were served dinner. Whereas, we were warned off even attempting to dock at the next restaurant downstream, which now preferred its clientele to arrive by helicopter rather than boat.

Day Three: Moulsford to Sonning

On leaving Moulsford, we soon came upon Cleeve Lock. As locks go, it is pretty enough, I'm sure. But in truth, no matter how picturesque they were to behold from the bank, I always experienced a sense of dread as we manoeuvred our small, vulnerable craft through the entrance and the great wooden gates swung shut. Then the water poured out through the sluices and we dropped into the gloom. As we slid down the wet mossy walls lined with thick chains, it was like descending into a dungeon. There was an anxious wait till the water settled and the far gates creaked slowly open, releasing us back into the sunlight.

The river below Cleeve is a fine stretch to row, with wide sweeping bends and tree-lined banks. Then on to Pangbourne, where we stopped for lunch at the Swan. As we proceeded further down river, we increasingly encountered fellow river travellers. They basically belonged to one of three classes, neatly encapsulating England's social

strata. There were the proletariat, the longboats, which had somehow strayed from their natural habitat of the industrial canals. Long, thin and gloomy, they looked like northern terraced housing. Their drivers stood stoically in all weathers at the exposed rear tiller, mug of tea in hand, clad in their underwear and wellies, while their wan-faced female companions peered through the net-curtained portholes. Then there were the nouveau riches, the large gleaming motor launches. Built for ocean crossings but confined inland, they patrolled angrily up and down the Thames like armoured tanks. Their owners, bare-chested with gleaming gold medallions, stood cocky and sure behind big brass steering wheels, while at the front, their blond blousy mistresses sunned their cellulite, like prow heads designed by Beryl Cook. And top of the hierarchy, indifferent to it all, were the sleek Edwardian motor launches, made of polished timber, recalling a distant era.

Like their elderly but sprightly owners, with tanned angular faces and superior smiles.

We approached Reading where the banks are lined with boathouses. A scull flashed past us, going the other way. Four young females clad in matching tight white tops and shorts, their oars and bodies moving in and out, in perfect harmony. We watched transfixed. It was pure and distilled, and so highly erotic. Charged with endorphins, we flexed our biceps, adopted heroic looks and pulled muscular strokes. But the effect was badly spoiled when we hit Poplar Island, and were both thrown face first from our seats. The last I saw was the girls smiling sympathetically as they slipped into the haze.

For a while after that we rowed in a subdued silence. Through Reading. Past the Three Men in a Boat pub at Caversham Bridge. It was the only epitaph that I saw on the river to Jerome's adventure. Which was somewhat ironic given his views on the place. According to Jerome, Reading 'does its best to spoil and sully and make hideous as much of the river as it can reach. The river is dirty and dismal here. One does not linger in the neighbourhood of Reading.'

But shortly beyond Reading is the charming village of Sonning. In the hushed early evening we pulled beneath Sonning Bridge, the arches reflected in the channel as if in a mirror, and moored on the towpath.

Day Four: Sonning to Cookham

The next morning brought another fine day. After negotiating Shiplake Lock, we began the three mile pull up to Henley. It is a beautiful stretch of river. Huge country houses, with long striped lawns rolling down to the bank.

And then Henley itself, exuding a calm air of quintessential Englishness. The previous week had seen the regatta here. White markers stretched out on either side of us into the shimmering distance, and grandstands and marquees lined the bank. We were on the historic one-and-a-quarter mile (2 km) course. There was obviously nothing for it but to give it a go.

As the prow crossed the starting line, we picked up pace. Blades flashing, we cut through the water leaving a long trail of wake in our path. There are moments in rowing when you achieve a perfect sense of timing, when it becomes a truly majestic endeavour. And we were in that state of grace. I looked up expectantly for the finishing post. 'One Mile' read the marker. Meaning one mile still to go. When we finally broached the line at Temple Island, we fell spent on our oars. Our time was 16 minutes and 10 seconds. It was a heroic effort. If some way off the time of 7 minutes and 5 seconds with which Pinsent and Cracknell had won the Silver Goblets and Nickall's Challenge Cup in the preceding week.

Thereafter we proceeded at a more leisurely pace, past Bisham Abbey, once home to Anne of Cleves and Queen Elizabeth I, but now a national sporting centre. We exchanged insults with a rowing boat blocking the centre channel, ineptly manned by four tattooed youths, who were probably the national football team.

Then at Marlow Lock we were almost overrun by an armada heading upriver, pennants and flags brazenly flying. The vessels came in all shapes and sizes — open, closed, sculled and motored — but all carried crews bedecked in neat uniforms of blazers and flannels. It was the Swan Uppers. On their annual outing to 'up' the swans. To count them, tag them and claim ownership of them for their respective patrons, the Queen, the Vintners or the Dyers. It is, even as quaint old English events go, quite a baffling affair.

That night we moored under Cookham Bridge and walked the couple of miles into town, where we spent the night at the Old Swan Uppers. I called my sister who was confined to bed with an illness. As she bitterly lamented her bad luck, missing the finest week in England for decades, I smugly consoled her and wished her well. A few minutes later she phoned back. There was a new-found cheer in her voice. She had just heard a weather forecast predicting a storm of biblical proportions. Flooding was expected on the Thames. She already sounded a lot better. The news had done her the world of good.

Day Five: Cookham to Runnymede

We awoke and peered out nervously. Clear blue sky. We laughed and cheerily set off for the river. But an hour later the sky was black with rage and the air hung heavy with impending violence. As we rowed down Cliveden Reach, beneath the great house, it was with a nervous foreboding.

There was a loud roar, a tearing flash, and the sky split open to unleash a torrent. Rain came down in blinding sheets, stinging my skin. The river's surface was violently puckered, as if strafed by machine gun fire. Within an instant, everything and everywhere was wet.

The downpour eased when we stopped for lunch at Bray. And then recommenced with fresh vigour as soon as we were back in the boat. We passed through a sodden

Windsor, by a flooded racecourse and dark gloomy castle. Through a drenched Eton and the dank woods of the Queen's Estate. Thick, heavy raindrops drummed and rebounded off the river. Inches of water lay in the bow. This was not fun.

But then, almost as abruptly as it had started, the rain stopped, the clouds parted and the sun burst through, alighting the dripping trees. We decided to set up camp and scrambled up the steep bank, into Runnymede National Trust Park. As JB tended the stove, I sat contemplating the small wooded island opposite, where the recalcitrant King John had been forced at sword point to sign the *Magna Carta*. It seemed an unprepossessing place to have hosted liberation from the crown.

I was interrupted from my historical musings by a gruff officious voice. 'Camping is not permitted here', it said.

I turned to find the uncompromising face and uniform of a park keeper. 'We're not camping', I replied, bolstered by my historic liberties. 'We're staying on our boat.'

'What boat?' enquired the park keeper bemused, and perhaps justifiably, for a quick scan of the horizon revealed no vessel.

'That one', said JB, pointing down past our feet, to where our small craft was tied.

'Oh', said the park keeper, with a mixture of disappointment and pity. 'Oh', he repeated, and left.

After the deluge came a glorious evening, the wet grass and trees glinting in the sunlight. Families of swans paraded up and down the river, perfectly aligned in order of height. It was as if the parents were proudly displaying their offspring to us. But they were probably just trying to restore their dignity, after their ordeal at the hands of the Uppers.

Day Six: Runnymede to Richmond

I awoke to a dull grey morning, the river's surface dimpled with rain. JB sat hunched on the river bank, muttering dark oaths, as he fruitlessly tried to light the stove. From the low clouds overhead came the unrelenting drone of airplanes into and out of Heathrow. We decided we had had enough, dumped our gear on board, and set out to row the remaining twenty-one miles (34 km) home.

After just over a mile (1.5 km) we passed under the M25. To the continual drone of airplanes was now added the perpetual whine of cars. We had crossed a portal. We had left behind rural England and re-entered London's grim orbit. The river was a sluggish, curdled green. The banks were lined with ugly houseboats. And the housing suddenly looked affordable. We were firmly back in our own world.

We rowed steadily on towards Teddington, with an eye on the clock, for we had been warned not to venture below here after 5pm. Thereon the Thames is tidal, and though it is only two miles downstream to Richmond, it is a Herculean task if you are pulling against the tide. As the afternoon progressed and time ticked by, our pace became more frantic, like young virgins caught out in Transylvania as dusk approaches.

We struck Teddington at 4pm and decided to press on. Teddington Lock is a forbidding place, the biggest on the river, with the deepest drop. Three separate locks cater for different-sized vessels, the Skiff Lock disquietingly known as the Coffin. And it is aptly named. On my previous excursion on the Thames, on a picnic jaunt from Richmond, I had managed to sink our rowing boat here when the rowlock had caught in the ladder. As the sluice gates opened and the water flooded in, we had abandoned our posts in panic and watched from above, in horrified fascination, as the boat disappeared from view and then a flotsam of cushions and sandwiches floated to the surface. It was therefore with some apprehension that I ventured into the Coffin again. But this time I emerged unscathed and, when the gates swung open to release us, we were on the final stretch home.

We decided to finish in style, with athletic aplomb. It would cap the trip. And JB thought that his girlfriend might have come down to see us in. After our week on the river, we were now a polished outfit, a well-oiled machine.

Our bodies arched together and our oars sliced the water in unison. But unfortunately we were not moving forward. The tide had turned.

As we strained and struggled to pull the lumbering craft downriver, rubbish caught in the current roared past us in the opposite direction. The boat continually slewed across the river to the outer bank. Over my shoulder, in the drizzle, I could see our destination of Richmond Bridge getting gradually further away. We increased the stroke count and desperately urged each other on. Finally, aching and breathless, we struggled in under the bridge and clattered into the boat-owner's pontoon. That last mile had taken close on an hour: our slowest on the river by far.

That evening we toasted our adventure, weary but satisfied. It had been a splendid trip. It had taken us through some of the most beautiful parts of our country and we had felt the touch of history. I felt proud and privileged. And I wasn't going to let my mood be spoiled by having just read the concluding chapter of *Three Men in a Boat*, in which Jerome dismisses the notion of making the journey downstream, with the current in one's favour, as being only for 'folk too constitutionally weak, or too constitutionally lazy'.

Footnote: single, double and treble sculling skiffs can be hired from Thames Skiff Holidays, Richmond (Tel 0208 844 2580; ask for Tom Balm). The hire of a double camping skiff for a week, including its transportation to Oxford, cost £315.

RICHARD WHEELER

The Gutenberg legacy

IN 1455, IN THE SMALL TOWN OF MAINZ IN GERMANY, A NEW edition of the Bible went to press. By today's standards the print run was hardly spectacular: only 180 copies all told. It was nonetheless a grand undertaking, its two volumes containing a total of 1,282 pages, with each page composed of two 42-line columns of text and embellished with richly coloured initial letters and borders. Hundreds of years have passed since this Bible first appeared, and yet for many the perfection and beauty of its printed page, and the achievement of its creation, remain unsurpassed. Today fewer than fifty copies survive, but it is known to many, for it carries the name of the genius whose supreme legacy it remains: the Gutenberg Bible.

The very great importance of the Gutenburg Bible lies in the fact that its creation marks the birth of printing in Western Europe. Prior to 1455, letters of type had to be individually engraved or cast, an expensive and time-consuming process. Then, midway through the fifteenth century, Johannes Gutenberg invented a way of mechanising the production of printing type. The significance of this breakthrough is hard to exaggerate. At a sweep the means of book production were radically democratised; books could be turned out far more quickly, for far less money, by a far greater cross-section of society.

Nowadays, in spite of the proliferation of alternative technologies, the printed word is in the rudest of health. No corner of our lives is immune: books, newspapers, magazines, advertisements, leaflets and letters, bills and bank statements. The printed word is there at the beginning of life and at the end, on birth and death certificates. But while the word itself proliferates, older printing technologies — descendents of those once employed by Gutenberg and England's own prototypographer, William Caxton — have not fared well, swept aside by the likes of ink-jet, laser and lithographic printing.

The outlook for older printing technologies would seem bleak, were it not for a small but significant number of independent publishers and hobby printers, determined not to let traditional printing techniques or methods of book production disappear, or the related knowledge and skills dissipate.

There are currently perhaps sixty private presses operating in the UK. All are small operations, often run by just a single person. Many have intriguing names: the Inky Parrot Press, the Strawberry Press and the Alembic Press to name just three. Their premises include workshops, sheds, barns, attics and other rooms 'taken over' by equipment. The books printed contrast with their mass-produced cousins in every conceivable way. Print runs are typically short, from a handful of copies up to a few hundred; the paper used is often made by hand, sometimes in a mould; type is set by hand, often in a number of colours; endpapers marbled by hand, bindings stitched by hand, and illustrations created, finished or coloured by hand.

Unsurprisingly, the subject matter too is extremely diverse, ranging from new versions of well-known works, to editions containing previously unseen prose, poetry and illustrations. In both cases, the low print runs, craft ethic and less pressing commercial demands allow — indeed positively encourage — the publication of subject matter of often dazzling originality, as well as the use of a boundless variety of formats and materials. The resulting books are often characterised by their eclecticism and inventiveness.

One such press — the Alembic — was established by Claire Bolton in 1972, and is now based in rural Oxford-shire having previously operated out of Edinburgh and Winchester. Claire was joined six years ago by her husband David, following his early retirement from work as a registrar in Oxford. The evolution of the Alembic Press mirrors that of many other private presses: a keen interest in printing quickly turned into a paying hobby which — through gradual modest expansion, and the acquisition of more equipment and founts of type — became a fully-fledged small business.

The current home of the Alembic Press could hardly be more suited to the needs of a small printing operation. Adjacent to a thirteenth-century farmhouse, Claire and David work from a stone barn which houses in one end the printshop and bindery, and in the other the type foundry. The former is very much the domain of Claire, while the type foundry is home to David. Each is a veritable Aladdin's Cave, stuffed full of all manner of printing and typecasting equipment, some old, some more recent; founts of type in wood and metal and any number of sizes and styles; assorted papers and cards, washing lines to hang newly-printed pages to dry, ink rollers, oil cans and wrenches, and all the other less easily-identifiable paraphernalia of the printer's art.

The print shop of the Alembic boasts not one press, but five: an Albion hand press, dating from 1866; Arab and Peerless Treadle presses, also dating from the nineteenth century; and Vandercook and Farley proof presses, the former dating from the 1950s and the latter from nobody seems to know quite when. Each press has its strengths and weaknesses, their especial foibles and joys which lend to each its unique character. The Albion, for example, consists of a bed on which the type lies waiting to be inked. At one end of this bed is a hinged frame, attached to which is a single sheet of paper. At the other end stands the powerful press mechanism itself. Once the paper has been inked and dropped onto the type, the bed glides on rails into the mouth of the press, a lever is pulled and the page is printed. This press is particularly well-suited to larger pages, but requires both considerable skill with the roller to ensure that the ink is applied evenly, and know-how to ensure that the pressure applied is neither too light, nor too heavy.

Built almost 100 years after the attractive Albion, the Vandercook provides it with a striking counterpoint. No concessions were made by its designers to those of a more aesthetic bent. Here function rules the day. Electrically powered oscillating rollers ensure a very even application of ink, while the paper is clamped around another roller, which ensures printing of very great accuracy. Unsurprisingly, printing with the Vandercook is faster, but the Albion has the advantage of being able to handle larger paper sizes.

Meanwhile, in the other half of the barn is David's workshop, containing equipment for the casting of type: a 1956 Monotype Super caster and two Monotype Composition casters. The nineteenth-century engineering of these contraptions is of mind-bending ingenuity, the process of casting the type itself almost miraculous. It begins with the text to be printed being typed out on a keyboard. This produces a punchtape which is then fed into one of the casters. The intricacies of the caster mechanism translate the holes in this tape into the movements along X and Y axes of a dye cast containing all of the matrices for the typeface being used. As each new letter is called for, the dye cast moves to the exact position over a small nozzle, up through which is forced molten lead. The newly-cast letter is pushed aside and the next is cast. As each line is completed it takes its place on the galley until the whole text — or galley proof — has been cast. Incredibly, a casting speed of up to 120 twelve-point characters per minute is possible.

With this array of equipment, allied to a freedom from the constraints that effectively hamstring commercial publishers, the printer is limited only by his or her imagination. At the Alembic, this freedom is most clearly expressed in an almost playful desire to experiment with formats and materials; a boundless curiosity that often leads to the creation of books that neither look nor behave as one expects a book to.

Recently, four miniature books were published at the Alembic, each measuring three inches (7.5 cm) square, and taking as their inspiration the garden during each of the four seasons. When the first of these — *Spring Garden* — is opened, the pages actually burst out to greet the reader; in the second — *Summer Garden* — the pages are folded concertina-fashion, with each fold at 90° to the next, so that the reader has to follow the winding course of a garden path as the book is unfolded. Here the ambling, spiralling text is illuminated by hand-coloured illustrations, and when the book is fully opened and turned over a large linocut of a poppy is revealed. *Autumn Garden* is in a 'Jacob's Ladder' format, and here the pages (which are over-printed with leaves) tumble out of the book.

Even the most cursory glance at the title lists of private presses reveals too just how rich is the variety of subject matter to be found. Certainly one can find poetry and prose by well-known writers, but when the impulse to commit to paper something more unusual is felt, a laudable fearlessness seems to surface again and again. This flexibility, to publish both the familiar and the highly personal, is well illustrated by the example of the Old Stile Press, based in Monmouthshire.

Like the Alembic, this press is run by a husband and wife team: Frances and Nicolas McDowall. In 2002, the couple published a copy of Wordsworth's famous poem, 'Tintern Abbey'. Living not far from the spot for fifteen years, and having felt a strong affinity with the poem long before moving to the area, it made an obvious choice. The final book contained the poem along with photographs taken in the area. It was printed on hand-made paper using spring water intercepted on its way to the Wye, and features endpapers incorporating plants found by the side of the stream.

Though a highly personal version of the poem, this was essentially the reprinting of a familiar text. However, looking down the list, another book grabs the eye, one whose contents could not be called familiar. During walks in Tintern Forest, Nicolas came upon a stretch of ancient wall.

'It had been on both sides of what seemed an imposing, if now overgrown, road leading away from the path on which we walked, curving left and out of sight. I have returned to the wall many times. The forest at that point has its own intense stillness, but the wall holds a fascination for me. The interlocking stones and the shadows between them form patterns which I found I could contemplate timelessly and I imagined somehow that great truths were for the unlocking. Where, though, was the key?'

The subsequent book, entitled *A Wall in Wales, An Observation*, and published in 1991, was Nicolas's attempt to answer this question.

This, in essence, is what makes the books produced by private presses so engaging: the unmistakable imprint of the printer's hand in everything; the clear record — there in black and white, in leather and paper, in words and pictures — of the choices that constitute a self-portrait of that maker. The continued existence of private presses speaks a simple truth that we knew all along: namely that the means we employ to express something are so telling and valuable an expression in their own right that their maintenance becomes imperative.

The mechanisation of the production of printing type was Gutenberg's particular gift to the world. Today the practice of letterpress lies once more in the hands of the few, but there are many reasons to be optimistic for its future. In the UK, interest in traditional printing remains solid, and the British Printing Society was joined in 1997 by a new organisation: the Fine Press Book Association. Meanwhile, in the United States, interest has burgeoned, particularly among the young. Ironically it may be the internet — the paperless medium — that has done more to disseminate knowledge of the still little-known art of letterpress printing.

Some small press websites:
Alembic Press website — full of interesting links:
    http://members.aol.com/alembicprs.
Fine Press Book Association — also full of interesting material and links:
    www.the-old-school.demon.co.uk/fpba/fpba.htm.
British Printing Society: www.bpsnet.org.uk.
Old Stile Press: www.oldstilepress.com.

WILLIAM BARRIE

Life amid the mountains

IN MY EARLY TEENS, WHEN I COMPLETELY LACKED THE CONFIDENCE to believe that beautiful girls might find me worth their precious time, I gave my heart to the Scottish mountains.

I still remember the first moment I saw in the distance the snow-covered hills of the Central Highlands. My heart caught in my throat. Now, more than forty years later, I realise with some sadness how seldom that has happened in my life. Those Scottish mountains became the landscape of my heart and largely remain so despite a lifetime of travel.

Not that they were or are easy friends. Being mountains, they attract a lot of rain and snow. Nothing quite matches the gloom of arriving in a cherished Highland glen to see the hills completely obscured and the mist rolling along the road and riverbed. Glencoe isn't the only glen of weeping. And nothing chills the spirit like falling waist deep in bog water on an interminably long approach walk, where the cherished mountain top seems to recede further and further the harder you press forward. I have

[134]

several friends who were forced to walk the Scottish hills in their school days and still keep alive a burning hatred of the place. But like many a love affair, apparent rejection only added to the attraction. When the weather was fine, the mountains were beautiful beyond belief.

So when my father died, the Scottish hills seemed the most natural place to go to rid myself of a sore heart and a heavy spirit.

—

Dad and I only got to know each other really well in the last few years of his life. I remember the day the friendship started. He was nearly seventy and I was exactly half his age. He wrote me a letter — most unusual — and it began: 'Whatever may have come between us in the past, I thought you should know that mother is not well and in hospital. You know you are always welcome to visit us, but if you can't or don't want to I will understand.'

By the time I got to the hospital, mother was in a coma from which she never recovered. Father and I found ourselves thrown together for three months of hospital visits and home routines. Bizarrely, they were days that had more than their share of happy and very funny moments.

Mother was in Glasgow's Western Infirmary, which specialises in brain surgery, for she had had a blood clot on the brain. The hospital was full of black humour and backchat along with all the silly realities and pompous promises of a local election campaign. The nurses were tough and devoted. The brain surgeon who cared for my mother would often arrive at her bed unannounced and sit there listening for a few moments, as if waiting for some secret she still had to tell him. We did the same.

[135]

For the first time in our lives, father and I could talk truthfully about anything. No point in keeping secrets now. One day in the car on the way to hospital, we recalled some stupid family row from the past when he suddenly said, 'The truth is I just loved your mother and would have done absolutely anything I could to make her happy'. So there we were, not father and son any more, but just two men talking as equals about the accidents of their lives.

We scattered my mother's ashes on a lovely spot in Scotland's Lowland hills, and after that we met about once a month for a weekend, and slowly he pieced together for me the story of his own days and dreams.

When he visited me at my new flat in London, I was always absurdly nervous. He was fastidious and talented with his hands, and I feared he would laugh at my fumbling attempts to make a home of the place. Then one day he called in to inspect a new kitchen I had just fitted, and looked long and quietly around him. And when he said, 'Elephants could dance on them shelves', I felt childishly grateful — a man in his late thirties still delighted at his father's approval.

When I visited him in his tiny pensioner's cottage, I took a sleeping bag and made up a camp bed on the living-room floor. Being a former miner, his coal bunker was always full to overflowing, and each night at bedtime he lit an enormous fire so I wouldn't be cold in the night. I cherished those nights drinking by the fire with him. He never understood my liking for good wine, given that England had such fine beer at a fraction of the price.

One evening he went to bed, dropped into a peaceful sleep and never woke up. His brother, who phoned me with the news, said: 'It's around about the anniversary of your mother's death. He misses her. And he's happy that you two are getting along so well. I think he just felt he'd done enough.'

—

The Scottish mountains were the only place I wanted to go — and one mountain in particular, Buchaille Etive Mhor in Glencoe, where I had attempted my first 'serious' rock climb as a teenager. The south face of the mountain rises almost sheer out of Rannoch Moor at the southern entrance to Glencoe and I booked into a hotel within full sight of my intended route up the rock.

Next morning, I booked a local mountain guide. It was around twenty years since I had been anywhere near a mountain and the delights of London life had made me soft. I wanted a climbing companion who knew the ropes in every sense. True to form, the mist was rolling down the hillsides into the glen, but at least we had no great walk to reach the face of the mountain.

In truth, the mist offered its own protection. It hung around the rock face like a comfort blanket and I had no sense of height or isolation at all. About halfway up the mountain, though, the mist cleared completely and very quickly. Suddenly, I looked around and the whole great expanse of Rannoch Moor stretched out below us. In the long distance across the moor, I could just make out the snow-covered hilltops of the central Highlands that had caught my imagination so much as a teenager.

I was standing on a narrow ledge and there, for a fraction of a moment, the choice offered itself. It wasn't at all a suicidal impulse, but in the aftermath of my father's

death and the sudden end of that new friendship, my interest in the future was low. It was grief's subtle game.

Some time before that, I had written about the death of one of my great climbing heroes, Dougal Haston, who was caught by an avalanche while ski-ing near his home in the French Alps. Almost inevitably, journalists speculated that he had taken his own life. He was low down the mountain, and many commentators refused to believe that such an accomplished skier and mountaineer could be caught in an accident like that in such good conditions. Whatever the truth of it, he was indeed the sort of man to demand death on his own terms in a place that he truly loved.

But for me, in that fraction of a moment on Buchaille Etive Mhor, the mountain was a life giver. I took one look at the view and the impulse for life came flowing back as I had perhaps subconsciously hoped it would. I climbed up the next few holds to find the guide unpacking lunch. 'I thought we'd stop here and have a look at the view. What kept you?'

The voice of the British countryside

Founded in 1927, *The Countryman* is one of the oldest, most respected countryside magazines in the world. It appears every month and is read by over 80,000 people throughout Britain and overseas, who share its concerns for the countryside, the people who live and work in it, and its wildlife.

Take out a subscription to *The Countryman* and discover more about the British countryside. It is also worth remembering that a subscription is a wonderful gift for friends or family.

	1 YEAR	2 YEARS	3 YEARS
UK	£23.00	£44.00	£66.00
Overseas	£35.00	£67.00	£102.00

Name

Address

Postcode   Telephone

Length of subscription ☐ 1 year   ☐ 2 years   ☐ 3 years

To start with the next issue

TOTAL VALUE OF ORDER £

☐ I enclose a cheque/PO made payable to DALESMAN PUBLISHING Co Ltd

Please debit my ☐ Access ☐ Visa ☐ Mastercard ☐ Switch*

Card number

Expiry date   Valid from   *Issue number
                                            (if paying by Switch)

Signature

☐ Please tick if you do NOT wish to receive information from other companies which we feel may interest you.

Please return to:

Dalesman Publishing Co Ltd
Stable Courtyard
Broughton Hall
Skipton
North Yorkshire
BD23 3AZ
Tel 01756 701033
Fax: 01756 709671
www.thecountryman.co.uk
subscriptions@dalesman.co.uk

Photocopy this page if you do not want to cut out the coupon

THE Countryman

PINEWOODS OF THE BLACK MOUNT

Peter Wormell, wood engravings by Christopher Wormell

The story of the resilience of a few
small pinewoods in the Scottish
Highlands, and the flora and fauna
which these majestic trees support.
Also described is the exploitation
which almost resulted in their
annihilation, and their regeneration. Peter Wormell's evocative text is
complemented by Christopher Wormell's superb wood engravings.

*Standard (ISBN 0 9543993 1 5): cloth bound with printed front panel and gold
blocked on spine. Limited to 1,000 copies. £15.95. Special (ISBN 0 9543993 2 3):
quarter bound in Wassa goatskin, bookcloth sides, head and tail bands, with
matching slipcase. Limited to 100 numbered copies. £75 + £10 p&p.*

CHRISTOPHER WORMELL
Limited edition print offer

A special, hand printed, limited-edition
print of a Christopher Wormell wood
engraving, individually signed and
numbered by the artist. £75 inc p&p.

Further copies of this and the first
two *Countryman Companions* – with
contributions from Andrew Motion,
Peter Ackroyd, Richard Mabey, Hugh
Fearnley-Whittingstall, Max Hastings
and David Bellamy – can be ordered from
Dalesman Publishing Co Ltd, price £4.99
each plus postage (UK 70p/copy, Europe
£1.48/copy, Rest of World £2.22/copy).

**To place an order or find out more, phone
the Countryman credit card hotline on (+44) 01756 701033
or visit www.thecountryman.co.uk.**